Blessings
for Mothers

Published by Barbour Publishing, Inc., P.O. Box 719, Uhrichsville, Ohio
44683, www.barbourbooks.com

*Our mission is to publish and distribute inspirational products offering
exceptional value and biblical encouragement to the masses.*

 Member of the
Evangelical Christian
Publishers Association

Printed in India.

Blessings
for Mothers

BARBOUR
PUBLISHING

The Gift

*Every good and perfect gift is from above, coming
down from the Father of the heavenly lights.*

—JAMES 1:17 NIV

The gift of motherhood is a "good and perfect"
gift from the Lord. Unwrap it, and you will
discover a depth of love and commitment
surpassed only by the cross.

Best Friend, Mother

A mother's love is indeed the golden link that binds
youth to age; and he is still but a child, however
time may have furrowed his cheek, or silvered his
brow, who can yet recall, with a softened heart, the
fond devotion, or the gentle chidings of the best
friend that God ever gave us.

—CHRISTIAN NESTELL BOVEE

What's Your Name?

Wouldn't you like to call out your child's name
without stuttering through the first syllables of all
your other children's names before finally landing on
the correct one? Thankfully, the Lord never bungles
your name nor confuses you with anyone else.
Rejoice that He knows you by name.

A Time to Laugh

Laughter is the shortest distance between two people.

—VICTOR BORGE

Is there distance between you and your children? Has life become too serious? If so, grab a book of corny jokes or rent a video of Christian comedians and let loose with some laughter. It's time to laugh.

Christlike

*God sends children to enlarge our hearts,
and make us unselfish and full of kindly
sympathies and affections.*

MARY HOWITT

Not only does God fill us with so much love
for our children it seems our hearts cannot
contain it, but He also uses our kids to help
us be selfless, sympathetic, and kind.
In other words, more Christlike.

Share

Seems like we tell our children a zillion times
a day to share their toys or their candy. But as
moms, we are also to share with our kids. . .things
like compassion, forgiveness, wisdom, laughter,
truth, integrity, optimism, godliness, faithfulness,
kindness, love, and *Jesus*. Remember, it's nice to
share.

He Is God

A common saying espouses, "God could not be everywhere, therefore He made mothers." A better adage is, "The mothers God made can't be everywhere, but that's okay because God *can*." His ability to be everywhere is one of the attributes that makes Him God. Rest in His omnipresence today.

Everlasting Forgiveness

*God pardons like a mother, who kisses the offense into
everlasting forgiveness.*

—HENRY WARD BEECHER

Be reminded today that in the same way you are able
to forgive your child forever and completely because
you love him, your loving God forgives you as well.
Forever and completely.

It Takes Courage

*Courage is what it takes to stand up
and speak; courage is also what it takes to
sit down and listen.*

—WINSTON CHURCHILL

Sometimes we mothers have to speak our
minds, but perhaps more often, we just
need to listen to our kids. It does take
courage, but joy and understanding
come in hearing their hearts.

Troublemakers

My mother had a great deal of trouble with me,
but I think she enjoyed it.

—MARK TWAIN

Unless their halos glow more brightly than most,
your children probably cause you a bit of trouble
now and then. But whether they are difficult or
delightful, appreciate them for who they are.

Matched Set

Have a mirror handy? Take a look and you will see
the mother God chose for your child. Now have your
child look in the mirror and tell her that she is seeing
the image of the child God chose especially for you.
It's a match made in heaven!

A Happy Home

Happy the home when God is there,
And love fills every breast;
When one their wish, and one their prayer,
And one their heavenly rest.
Happy the home where Jesus' name
Is sweet to every ear;
Where children early speak His fame,
And parents hold Him dear.

—HENRY WARE JR.

Truth

*It is one thing to show a man that he is in error,
and another to put him in possession of truth.*

—JOHN LOCKE

It is easy to point out our children's errors. But if
we also point them to God's truth, we equip them
to make wiser choices in the future. And
directing them to His love will help
them *want* to.

Faith and Hope

Pride is one of the seven deadly sins; but it cannot be the pride of a mother in her children, for that is compound of two cardinal virtues—faith and hope.

—CHARLES DICKENS

Faith—believing what you cannot see; and hope—an optimistic expectation. . . What would mothering be without them? Impossible.

Do the Impossible

You must do the thing you think you cannot do.

—ELEANOR ROOSEVELT

Today, maybe that "thing" was just to coerce your
sleep-deprived body from your warm bed and plunk
your exhausted feet on the floor. Celebrate your
accomplishment and, in God's strength, face your
other impossibilities with faith and confidence.

For Now

I awoke this morning
At three o'clock
To crying in my ears.
I calmed my child
Tucked her in
Then thought of all the years
Of diaper changes
Newborn cries
Feedings in the night
And told myself
Someday I'll sleep
But for now I'll hold her tight.

Good Advice

Do all the good you can, in all the ways you can,
to all the souls you can, in every place you can,
at all the times you can, with all the zeal you can,
as long as ever you can.

—JOHN WESLEY

What an extraordinary approach to life to
teach our children—especially
by example.

Your Children—His Creation

Among the many acts of gratitude we owe to God, it may be accounted one to study and contemplate the perfections and beauties of His work of creation. Every new discovery must necessarily raise in us a fresh sense of the greatness, wisdom, and power of God.

—JONATHAN EDWARDS

Hope

Hope transcends our current circumstances,
elevating us above sibling rivalry, marital issues,
financial strain, dirty dishes, and sleep deprivation by
declaring, "This ain't all there is!" and "Something better
is coming!" Jesus Christ, in whom the Christian's hope
resides, certainly transcended His circumstances
and gave us hope when He defeated death.
Something better was definitely coming!

Never Apart

*She never quite leaves her children at home,
even when she doesn't take them along.*

—MARGARET CULKIN BANNING

Once you are a mother, your children become
such a part of you that you take them with you
everywhere—even when they're really home with
Dad feasting on caffeinated soda and dessert before
dinner.

Don't Give Up!

Let us not lose heart in doing good, for in due time we will reap if we do not grow weary.

—GALATIANS 6:9 NASB

In other words, hang in there! Keep the faith! Don't give up! Finish the race! And it sure can't hurt to take a nap, either.

Lighten Up

A person without a sense of humor is like a wagon without springs. It's jolted by every pebble on the road.

—HENRY WARD BEECHER

When your parenting road becomes strewn with a pebble of miscommunication here or a stone of frustration there, a sense of humor can help smooth your way.

Limitless Love

*Maternal love: a miraculous substance
which God multiplies as He divides it.*

—VICTOR HUGO

I wondered if I would love my second child as much
as my first. I need not have worried, for love is not a
varying and measurable quantity, but rather a limitless
outpouring from God's heart. It cannot be used up!

Sowing and Reaping

Sow an act, reap a habit; sow a habit, reap a character;
sow a character, reap a destiny.

—GEORGE DANA BOARDMAN

The Bible teaches that we reap what we sow. As
mothers, we have awesome opportunities to sow acts
that will shape our children's destinies in a positive
manner. Let us sow wisely.

Just Because

I love these little people; and it is not a slight thing when they, who are so fresh from God, love us.

—CHARLES DICKENS

It is a wondrous thing that God sent a little person who loves you not because of how wonderful you are, but just because you *are*. Sounds like the same reason God loves you.

It's You

Be who you are and be that well.

—ST. FRANCIS DE SALES

The next time you catch yourself gazing upon the astonishing feats of other moms and feeling worse than inadequate, know this: You are only supposed to be *you*, the person God made you to be. *You* are who your kids need.

The Real Thing

*A real Christian is a person who can
give his pet parrot to the town gossip.*

BILLY GRAHAM

Although humorous, this statement has a lot to say
about integrity. Are we the same moms at home as we
are in public? God, help us to be authentic.

Mom Classified

Wanted: Mature, self-disciplined, entertaining,
focused, articulate, energized, organized, wise,
patient, multi-tasking, enthusiastic teacher
with theological, psychiatric, culinary, medical,
engineering, and secretarial training. Must operate
multiple household appliances, locate lost items,
and kiss boo-boos. Benefits—unlimited. Vacation—
never. Retirement package—someday, if job done
correctly. Flexible applicants only, please.

Greatest Privilege

*Life affords no greater responsibility,
no greater privilege, than the raising of the
next generation.*

— C. EVERETT KOOP

Your children will eventually become adults.
What you teach them now and how you lead
them now will affect the future in ways you
may never know. Make it count!

Who Are You?

*The best way to find yourself is to lose
yourself in the service of others.*

—INDIRA GHANDI

Motherhood is a high calling that requires lowly
acts of service. When you completely give yourself
over to the demands—and rewards—of mothering,
though, you discover who God intends you to be.

If Babies Could Talk

"What's your hurry, Mom? Let's snuggle a little longer."
"Sorry about the spit-up and leaky diaper thing. Really."
"Sleep is overrated."
"What *is* that stuff in those little jars anyway?"
"I love you."
"You know that 'Jesus Loves Me' thing? It goes for you,
      too, Mom."

DAY 32

Tiny Teachers

What instruction the baby brings to the mother!
—THOMAS WENTWORTH HIGGINSON

What have you learned from your baby? Maybe patience, perseverance, sacrifice. . .and how to survive on minuscule amounts of sleep? If we are teachable, God can use the privilege of motherhood to help us grow in our Christian walk.

Praise Him

God has given you your child, that the sight
of him, from time to time, might remind you of
His goodness, and induce you to praise Him
with filial reverence.

—CHRISTIAN SCRIVER

When you are lost in the wonder of the
miracle that is your child, praise your
heavenly Father. He is worthy.

Gift of Life

Take a moment to reflect on the gift of life. When God gave you the title "mother," He invited you to participate in one of His most amazing miracles: the growth and development of another human being. And the slobbery kisses and dandelion bouquets are just a bonus.

Childish Perspective

There is a garden in every childhood, an enchanted place where colors are brighter, the air softer, and the morning more fragrant than ever again.

—ELIZABETH LAWRENCE

The innocence and natural wonder of children cause them to see the world from a perspective of awe and appreciation for God's creation. Maybe we should look through their eyes.

No Compromise

If you just set out to be liked, you would be prepared to compromise on anything at any time, and you would achieve nothing.

—MARGARET THATCHER

The world needs kids raised to focus not on persuading people to like them, but on doing the right thing, every time, no matter the cost.

Free to Fly

*There are only two lasting bequests
we can hope to give our children.
One is roots; the other, wings.*

—HODDING CARTER

It may seem paradoxical, but *grounding* our
children—in God's truth, that is—actually
grants them wings with which to soar
through life in freedom and security.

Love Lesson

Lord, thank You for blessing me beyond my imagination, especially for my beautiful family whom I love so deeply and completely. It is through my love for them that You are revealing the depth of Your love for me. Thank You for this love lesson. Please teach it to my children, as well. Amen.

Blessing Giver

*There never was a person who did anything worth doing,
who did not receive more than he gave.*

— HENRY WARD BEECHER

Mothers give so much of their time, energy (physical,
emotional, mental, spiritual), talents, and love,
it's hard to imagine receiving back more in the form of
blessings. That's because Christ's ability to give is simply
greater than our ability to imagine.

Sanctuary

Some days you feel like Mother of the Year. . .and other days, well, you don't. On those less-than-wonderful days, you probably want to resign and hide away on a deserted, tropical island. But since quitting is not a viable option, remember you can always run to the sanctuary of God's presence. Hide in Him!

Good Medicine

Does your broken spirit need a repair? Is your heart in need of a spiritual transfusion? Proverbs 17:22 teaches, "A joyful heart is good medicine" (NASB). Ask your heavenly Father to fill you and your family with His joy—the kind of medicine that tastes sweet to the soul.

He Can

As a mother, my job is to take care of what is possible and trust God with the impossible.

—RUTH BELL GRAHAM

Some days, none of what is put before you may seem possible. Remember, though, that the God who fed thousands with a few loaves and fish is Lord over the impossible. Nothing is too big for Him.

To My Children

Jesus loves *you*, this I know, for the Bible tells me so.
I cannot comprehend how Jesus can love you more
deeply than I, but I know He does. Perhaps He knows
more about how to truly love. After all, what manner
of love was required to endure the cross?

Richer Than Gold

You may have tangible wealth untold;
Caskets of jewels and coffers of gold.
Richer than I you can never be—
I had a mother who read to me.

—STRICKLAND GILLILAN

Snuggle up together and read. You and your kids will always treasure the time and the stories.

Self-Taught

*There's nothing that can help you understand
your beliefs more than trying to explain them to
an inquisitive child.*

—FRANK A. CLARK

They say if you want to learn something,
teach it. That certainly holds true in
parenting. If you are going to explain why
you believe a certain way, you will solidify
your reasons first so you are able
to articulate them.

True Love

Nothing is sweeter than love, nothing stronger, nothing higher, nothing broader; nothing is more lovely, nothing richer, nothing better in heaven or in earth.

—THOMAS À KEMPIS

People overuse the word "love" quite often—they "love" pizza or they "love" a certain movie. But authentic love in its truest form is a portrait of God. Because God *is* love.

Relax

Parenting. . . If you fear you've done it all wrong,
and that society—or at least your child's future
spouse—will suffer for it, take a deep breath, pray,
and trust God to fill in the gaps and redeem your
mistakes. After all, your perfect heavenly Father
knows exactly what each child needs.

Prayer Treasure

*I remember my mother's prayers and they have
always followed me. They have clung
to me all my life.*

—ABRAHAM LINCOLN

You can do no sweeter or more powerful thing for
your children than pray for them. And when you
pray *with* them, you teach them how to pray,
and they will treasure your words always.

Sound Familiar?

If you talk like this: Don't-tape-your-sister's-mouth-shut-I-don't-know-what's-for-dinner-get-out-of-the-dryer-I'm-in-the-bathroom-can-it-wait-hurry-we're-late-who-took-a-shower-with-the-curtain-open-why-is-there-a-snowball-in-the-freezer-you-did-*what?* Then you might be a mom.

Heartfelt

*The best and most beautiful things in the world cannot be
seen or even touched. They must be felt within the heart.*

—HELEN KELLER

Seeing and holding our children are marvelous
blessings. But the intangible rewards of
motherhood—intense love and profound joy that
fill the heart to overflowing—are greater still.

By Degrees

*How poor are they who have not patience! What wound did
ever heal but by degrees?*

—WILLIAM SHAKESPEARE

A patient mother understands that the process of
childrearing does not happen at once but comes about
"by degrees." And she finds joy in each degree.

See-Through

There are many ways to bless your children, but one of the most meaningful is to be transparent. Show them you don't have all the answers, but that you know Someone who does. By authentically seeking the Lord yourself, you help their faith move from their heads to their hearts, right where it belongs.

Love Motive

*We ought not to be weary of doing little
things for the love of God, who regards
not the greatness of the work, but the
love with which it is performed.*

—BROTHER LAWRENCE

When you fulfill your motherly responsibilities
with love as your motive, the Lord honors
your work and blesses you. In fact, you
might say He loves it when you love.

Like No Other

There is no friendship, no love, like that of the
parent for the child.

—HENRY WARD BEECHER

No other sentiment quite compares with the
affection, fondness, emotion, and tenderness
you feel for your child. . .nor the frustration,
disappointment, irritation, and exasperation.
But still, you love. Because you are a mother.

Building Blocks

We make a living by what we get;
we make a life by what we give.

—WINSTON CHURCHILL

A mother continually gives to her family, and through
that giving she builds not only her life, but the lives of
her children. Her building blocks? Faith,
sacrifice, commitment, character,
perseverance, wisdom, and love.

Character Lessons

*You can learn many things from children. How much
patience you have, for instance.*

—FRANKLIN P. JONES

Our children possess the ability to reveal the
sometimes-cavernous gaps in our character, as well
as a knack for creating situations in which we are
forced to acquire the qualities we lack. Character
lessons, anyone?

Fifteen Minutes Equals Forever

"How do you do the will of God for the rest of your life? You do it for the next fifteen minutes!" The revival preacher's words resonated in my mother's heart. How can I be a good mom forever? By being a good mom for the next fifteen minutes.

Safe at Home

Where we love is home—home that our feet may leave,
but not our hearts.

—OLIVER WENDELL HOLMES SR.

A loving mother helps create a place where the
child, in his heart, will always feel safe and attached
and loved. It is a trite saying, but home truly is
"where the heart is."

Seriously

"But Mom, you don't, like, understand!"
How many mothers have heard these words
from their teenage daughters? Ironically, it is the
child who doesn't understand, for she cannot
grasp the astonishing fact that her mother, who is
now very old, was, like, a *girl* at one time. Will
they ever get it that we *get it*? I mean, *seriously*.

Soul Imprint

The instruction received at the mother's knee, and the paternal lessons, together with the pious and sweet souvenirs of the fireside, are never effaced entirely from the soul.

—ABBE HUGO FELICITE DE LAMENNAIS

Your virtuous instruction and special memories leave their imprint on your child forever. What a privilege!

Talk About Him

In Deuteronomy 11:18–19, God instructs, "So commit yourselves completely to these words of mine. Tie them to your hands as a reminder, and wear them on your forehead. Teach them to your children. Talk about them when you are at home" (NLT). God's words are the best topic of conversation!

Day 62

Choose Love

To lead our children to Christ, we can choose from two approaches. One is to grab them by the shirt collar, self-righteously point them to the cross, and demand that they accept our faith. Or we can gently take them by the hand and lovingly lead them to the Savior, who longs for a relationship with them. Let's choose love.

God Is Goodness

*The goodness of God is infinitely more wonderful
than we will ever be able to comprehend.*

—A. W. TOZER

Just as God *is* love and God *is* kindness, He is also
goodness. And His goodness is an all-encompassing
characteristic of His personality that cannot be
separated from the rest of who He is. He is *God*,
and He is *goodness*.

A Mother's Prayer

Lord, use my words and my actions each day as brushes on a canvas to paint a portrait of You for my children. May they see the beautiful kaleidoscope of Your personality: Your creativeness, Your sensitivity, Your forgiveness, Your grace, Your compassion, Your wisdom, and Your unconditional love. Amen.

Unemployed

One of these days (if you haven't already),
you will find yourself in the unemployment
line. Not the government variety, but the line
formed by all the mothers who complete their
tasks of raising their children to adulthood.
A bittersweet stage for sure, but I hear the
unemployment benefits are amazing!

Pass It On

*There are souls in this world which have their gift
of finding joy everywhere and of leaving
it behind them when they go.*

—FREDERICK WILLIAM FABER

What legacy will you leave your children? What
better heritage to impart to your children than one
of joy—deep, abiding, eternal joy. The kind that
only Christ can give.

Potential Within

*A rock pile ceases to be a rock pile the moment a
single man contemplates it, bearing within
him the image of a cathedral.*

—ANTOINE DE SAINT-EXUPÉRY

Your child is not just another kid. Within him lies the
potential for something magnificent, and as his mother,
you wisely and patiently seek to help him build it.

DAY
68

Keep On

Perseverance is a great element of success. If you only knock long enough and loud enough at the gate, you are sure to wake up somebody.

—HENRY WADSWORTH LONGFELLOW

Whether it is parenting for the long haul or literally attempting the feat of rousing your teenager from her bed, perseverance is the key. You keep walking, you keep knocking!

Good Read

*Judicious mothers will always keep in mind
that they are the first book read, and the last
put aside, in every child's library.*

—C. LENOX REMOND

What kind of book are you? Fiction?
Nonfiction? Devotional? Anthology?
Joke book? If much of our children's
development hinges on what they
"read" in us, let's enlist the Lord's help
to ensure we are a good read.

Asleep on the Job

Moms multi-task like no one else. We do laundry,
unload the dishwasher, corral the kids, take a phone
call, locate a lost shoe, help a child with schoolwork,
make a grocery list, and go through the mail, all
while cooking dinner. Imagine the possibilities
if we could just discover how to *sleep* while
accomplishing all this. . . .

Soft Touch

*Govern a family as you would cook a
small fish—very gently.*

—CHINESE PROVERB

Being gentle with your children means to handle
them carefully—not just physically, but
emotionally and spiritually, as well. Use a soft
touch and a softly spoken word when possible, and
assume they are doing the best they know how to do.
(This works well with husbands, too.)

In His Hands

A man traveling out of town asked God to take care of his children while he was away. God replied, "Who do you think takes care of them while you're here?" What a comforting reminder that even though we go to great lengths to ensure the safety and well-being of our children (and rightly so), the Lord is their supreme caretaker!

Lead by Example

He that gives good advice, builds with one hand;
he that gives good counsel and example, builds
with both; but he that gives good admonition
and bad example, builds with one hand and pulls
down with the other.

—FRANCIS BACON

Lord, help us build with both hands that we
would not destroy by our actions what
our words seek to build.

Too Much to Do?

A friend once advised: "There is always enough time in the day to do what God wants you to do, but not always enough time to do the things you think you should do." The key is to determine the difference. Prayerfully consider each responsibility or activity, and the Lord will help you distinguish which ones are truly from Him.

Peaceful Home

*He is happiest, be he king or peasant,
who finds peace in his home.*

JOHANN WOLFGANG VON GOETHE

Our homes are our sanctuaries from the world. When
we have a sanctuary to which we can retreat, a safe
haven where truth is valued and Christ's love reigns
supreme, we can muster what we need to keep going.
Home, sweet, *peaceful* home.

Smiley Face

Every time you smile at someone, it is an action of love, a gift to that person, a beautiful thing.

—MOTHER TERESA

A smile or frown can set the tone for the whole day, good or bad. Are there enough smiles in your home? Find a smile and share it with your children. It's a beautiful gift.

He Holds Tomorrow

Every tomorrow has two handles.
We can take hold of it with the handle
of anxiety or the handle of faith.

—HENRY WARD BEECHER

Motherhood is an incredibly daunting
task if we dwell on the physical,
emotional, and financial aspects of
raising a child. So let us take hold of
tomorrow with the "handle of faith,"
and leave it in God's hands.

Amidst a Miracle

With his minuscule fingers and toes, button nose, and dewy-soft skin, a baby is a wondrous miracle. But consider that your toddler, preschooler, elementary-aged child, and yes, even your teenager, are miracles, as well. Their capacity to learn and grow, laugh and love, talk (and talk back?) is limitless and miraculous. And you are part of the miracle!

Journey On

While reading to our children about God leading
the Israelites with pillars of cloud and fire, I doubted
Hannah (age five) was listening. I asked her, "What
were the Israelites supposed to do when the cloud or
fire moved?" She responded dramatically, "Journey on!"
You know, that's what we need to do, as well. With God's
leading, we *journey on*.

Only One

*The child must know that he is a miracle, that since the
beginning of the world there hasn't been, and until the end
of the world there will not be, another child like him.*

—PABLO CASALS

A child who understands his unique design will be
confident and secure and more likely to discover and
use his God-given gifts and abilities.

Finishing Touch

*I will cry to God Most High, to God
who accomplishes all things for me.*

—PSALM 57:2 NASB

This verse contains a life-changing declaration
for you, Mom: God will finish, complete,
perform, and perfect *everything* for you.
Trust the Lord to include your children
in this promise!

DAY
82

Glorify Him

When I stand before God at the end of my life, I would
hope that I would not have a single bit of talent left, and
could say, "I used everything You gave me."

—ERMA BOMBECK

When you use your gifts and talents for the Lord,
others are drawn to Him because of what they see
in you. Use all of them!

God's Instrument

Lord, make me an instrument of Your peace!
Where there is hatred, let me sow love;
Where there is injury, pardon;
Where there is doubt, faith;
Where there is despair, hope;
Where there is darkness, light;
Where there is sadness, joy.

—ST. FRANCIS OF ASSISI

Parenting Consultants

My teenagers give me so much parenting advice,
I tell them to write a book. When they bestow
their wisdom on why a decision or rule is wrong, I
jokingly ask, "What page will that be on?" Probably
taking a little too much delight in the prospect, I
want them to read their words *after* they become
parents—*of teenagers*!

Forgiving Family

*Humanity is never so beautiful
as when praying for forgiveness,
or else forgiving another.*

—JEAN PAUL

A family naturally creates a myriad of
situations that necessitate forgiveness.
Unintentional offenses, short tempers,
and disrespect can lose their power to
wound, though, if all involved seek
forgiveness from each other
and the Lord.

Oops!

Once there was a mom and boy outside visiting the dad next door. Suddenly, the little boy piped up with, "My dad says you guys are deadbeats 'cause you never put Christmas lights on your house!" The moral of this story? Children repeat what they hear so we'd better make sure they hear the right things!

God + Impossible = Possible

*Sometimes I've believed as many as six
impossible things before breakfast.*

—LEWIS CARROLL

Here are some suggestions: I *can* get up. My children
will get along today. Breakfast has been catered in. *(It
can happen.)* The house is *clean.* Jesus loves *me.*
He's *alive*! Remember that "impossible"
is not in God's vocabulary!

Future Effect

*Children are the living messages we
send to a time we will not see.*

—JOHN W. WHITEHEAD

Consider the influence you have on future
generations. For example, if you have three children,
and they each have three children, and so on down
the line, in a mere five generations, you will have
363 descendants. *You* can affect *their* world for
Christ!

Immanuel

The best of it is, God is with us.

—JOHN WESLEY

God didn't pitch you into the parenting boat then stand on the shore and wave, hollering, "Good luck! It's rough out there! Hope you make it!" No, Immanuel—*God with us*—climbed into the boat, took the helm, and whispered, "We will do this together. I am with you all the way."

Through Their Eyes

*Only those who look with the eyes of children can lose
themselves in the object of their wonder.*

—EBERHARD ARNOLD

If you see a dandelion as a lovely flower, and you
notice those tiny purple blossoms that grow in
the grass, and you gaze in wonder as an inchworm
crawls on your finger...then you "look with the eyes
of children."

Future Plans

We cannot always build the future for our youth, but we can build our youth for the future.

—FRANKLIN ROOSEVELT

Of course the future is in God's hands, but we can purposefully impart godly ideals such as wisdom, integrity, courage, and compassion. Then our children can make a kingdom difference when their future becomes their present.

Now

Your eyes are skimming these words, but are you really thinking about what you need to do next? Moms are usually so busy, they are physically in *this* moment but mentally already in the *next* one. To continually focus on what is next, though, means to miss what is *now*. Now is the time you have with your children. Enjoy it!

Refill, Please

Do you feel like a frayed shoelace hanging on by a lone thread? Or like an empty jar that others keep shaking for one more drop? Hanging on by a thread, nothing left to give...motherhood brings those times. Jesus desires to refill you—and keep you filled—at His bottomless well of love and provision. Just ask!

Good Woman, Mother

To be a good nurse one must be a good woman.
What makes a good woman is the better or higher or
holier nature: quietness, gentleness,
patience, endurance, forbearance. . . .

—FLORENCE NIGHTINGALE

The same qualities that make a "good woman"
likewise make a good mother. And your godly
motherhood is honorable and pleasing to God.

Some Things Other Moms Say (But Not You)

"Yes, my breath smells like chocolate. So?"

"Am I the only one who sees the dirty dishes and laundry?"

"Please don't talk to me while I'm on the phone. I appear to have an extra ear, but I cannot listen to two conversations."

"I don't have any idea what's for dinner!"

"Find all of your stuff yourself!"

DAY 96

Five Things You Would Like to Hear

"Dinner's ready, Mom. Did you enjoy your nap?"

"We're staying home tonight because we want to spend time with you."

"You should have your own cooking show! This is delicious!"

"Welcome home, Mom. How was the cruise?"

"The dishes are washed, the laundry is done, your bed is turned back. We love you! Good night!"

Holy Calling

And say to mothers what a holy charge
is theirs. With what a kingly power their love
might rule the fountains of the newborn mind.

LYDIA H. SIGOURNEY

Your child came ready to learn about
you, about the world, and about the Lord.
When God called you to motherhood, it
was a "holy charge" indeed.

Godly Mother

Mother, you built no great cathedrals
That centuries applaud,
But with a grace exquisite
Your life cathedraled God.

—THOMAS FESSENDEN

We are not expected to be perfect, but as mothers
we can exemplify the Lord by exhibiting godly
characteristics: peacefulness, forgiveness,
trustworthiness, dependability, faithfulness—
and a love that knows no limits.

Day 99

Master Carpenter

*The Christian home is the Master's workshop where the
processes of character molding are silently, lovingly,
faithfully, and successfully carried on.*

—LORD HOUGHTON

Imagine Jesus practicing His earthly father's trade
of carpentry, carefully and expertly molding a piece
of wood. Jesus is the Carpenter, your family is His
workshop, and you are one of His
specially chosen tools.

DAY
100

Family

The *consciousness of loving and being loved brings a warmth and richness to life that nothing else can bring.*

—OSCAR WILDE

The family is God's perfect atmosphere for love to be given and love to be received. It is also through the family that our lives are enriched as we are taught about His love for us.

God's Riches

By wisdom a house is built, and by understanding
it is established; and by knowledge the rooms are
filled with all precious and pleasant riches.

—PROVERBS 24:3–4 NASB

The Lord wants to give you wisdom,
understanding, and knowledge, and help you
create a loving home filled with "precious
and pleasant riches."

Mother

In her eyes the look of loving,
In her smile the warmth of caring.
In her hands the touch of comfort,
In her heart the gift of sharing.

—UNKNOWN

Lord, let my facial expressions and my touch radiate love and concern and comfort, and my heart pour out generosity and kindness. Amen.

Safe with Jesus

Who or what gives you a sense of self-worth? Perhaps your husband or children? Or maybe you work outside the home and receive affirmation through your job. Of course we want others to appreciate what we do, but Christ is the only true source for fulfillment and approval because He is unchangeable and dependable. Your "self" is safe with Him.

There Goes My Heart

Making a decision to have a child—it's momentous. It is to decide forever to have your heart go walking around outside your body.

—ELIZABETH STONE

You love your children so deeply that you feel their pain, sense their frustration, suffer their disappointment, experience their happiness, and enjoy their excitement as if it were all your own. Somehow it is!

Living and Loving

*You will find as you look back upon your life
that the moments when you have truly lived
are the moments when you have done things in
the spirit of love.*

—HENRY DRUMMOND

When you bandage a scraped knee,
comfort a sick child, prepare a meal
for your family, or help a child with
schoolwork, you are truly living.
Because you are loving.

Huh?

I know that you believe that you understood what you think I said, but I am not sure you realize that what you heard is not what I meant.

—ROBERT MCCLOSKEY

The next time you have a communication problem with loved ones, try this line. At worst, it will confuse them; and at best, it will lighten the mood. Either is good.

Well Done

*A mother is not a person to lean on,
but a person to make leaning unnecessary.*

—DOROTHY CANFIELD FISHER

As you teach and guide your children, they gradually take on more responsibility, and then eventually stand on their own. First you are a caretaker, then a personal trainer, then an advisor, then a spectator. And God will say, "Well done."

Mother, Teacher

The mother is and must be—whether she knows it or not—the greatest, strongest, and most lasting teacher her children have.

—HANNAH WHITALL SMITH

Throughout their lives, your children will be nurtured, discipled, and instructed by many people. But God, in His infinite wisdom, made *you* their mother, and your unique guidance will affect them like none other.

Everyday Miracle

Every day is a miracle when you are a mother.
How amazing it is that those little people
running around your house were created by
God and began life as microscopic specks of
humanity! They grow quickly, possess a zeal for
learning about God's creation, and love you just
because you're you. And they call you "Mom."
What a miracle.

More Than Duty

Duty makes us do things well,
but love makes us do them beautifully.

—PHILLIPS BROOKS

A hired servant could dutifully go through the motions and accomplish the same physical labor that you do as a mother. But your love for your family moves you from merely performing your duty to a higher dimension of selfless, unconditional, and beautiful service.

Always Good

Forming characters! Whose? Our own or others?
Both. And in that momentous fact lies the peril and
responsibility of our existence.

—ELIHU BURRITT

Not only are we largely responsible for the formation of
our children's character, but God graciously forms our
character in the process. Sometimes it is uncomfortable,
but it is always good for us.

DAY
112

Special Days

Our days are sometimes filled with warm fuzzies, happy children, and sappy sentiments. Other days we endure cold stares, grumpy children, and *snappy* sentiments. But every day, whether stress-free or stress-filled, is special in that our children will never again be as they are today, at this moment. Let's treasure the good, the bad, and the ugly!

Vital Role

The successful mother, the mother who does her part in rearing and training aright the boys and girls who are to be the men and women of the next generation, is of greater use to the community. . . . She is more important by far than the successful statesman or businessman or artist or scientist.

—THEODORE ROOSEVELT

Beautiful Ornament

*Mother—in this consists the glory
and the most precious ornament of woman.*

—MARTIN LUTHER

Just as a beautiful ornament adorns a Christmas
tree, your motherhood adorns your womanhood.
Just as the tree is still a tree without the ornament
but becomes lovelier by it, your femininity is
enhanced and beautified by your maternal love
and dedication.

Unconditional Love

Who is it that loves me and will love me forever with an affection which no change, no misery, no crime of mine can do away?—It is you, my mother

—THOMAS CARLYLE

You hold a deep, unchangeable love for your children. When they understand that you love them regardless, they also learn of God's unconditional love for them.

Power Supply

Do not pray for tasks equal to your powers.
Pray for power equal to your tasks.

—PHILLIPS BROOKS

An electrician first determines a building's electrical requirements then connects the house to the appropriate level of power. Likewise, we need to ensure our power level matches our tasks. Jesus is our power source. Let's get connected!

Together

After our house burned down, our family stayed two weeks in a hotel then moved to a rental house. It wasn't our house but we were still *home*. After six months, we moved to a different house and were home again. Each of the houses was temporary, but each was home because we were together as a family.

DAY 118

The Thing

The thing with motherhood is letting your kids go. The thing with kids is they want to spread their baby wings and fly before they're flight-tested. The thing with the world is it's just waiting to shoot them down. The thing with motherhood is letting them go . . .anyway. Trusting the Lord to protect them and help them fly? Now *that's* the thing.

DAY
119

The Present

*Cease to inquire what the future has in store,
and take as a gift whatever the day brings forth.*

—HORACE

Always trying to see around the corner keeps us from
focusing on the present. We cannot know what the
future holds, so why waste precious time dwelling on
it? We need to enjoy the present for the "gift" that it is.

It's All Love

*Some are kissing mothers and some are
scolding mothers, but it is love just the same.*

—PEARL S. BUCK

Under the umbrella of love, you practice a healthy
balance of affection and discipline. Because you
love your children, you discipline them. When you
discipline them, you demonstrate great affection to
show them the correction is born out of love.

Safe with the Shepherd

He tends his flock like a shepherd: he gathers
the lambs in his arms and carries them
close to his heart; he gently leads
those that have young.

—ISAIAH 40:11 NIV

Because you are precious to Jesus and
He loves you, He leads you and holds
you and your children close. Trust
the safety of His arms.

Day 122

Faith Fire

A mighty flame followeth a tiny spark.

—DANTE ALIGHIERI

Anger or bitterness can ignite an injurious flame you may be powerless to extinguish. On the other hand, a spark of enthusiasm or zeal for Christ can light a fire in a heart that burns through eternity. Let us kindle in our children an inextinguishable love for the Lord!

Beyond Us

What if our goals for our children centered not on making them our clones but helping them become better than us? Wouldn't it be grand if they turned out *more* generous, *more* considerate, *more* talented, *more* loving, and *more* passionate about Christ than we ourselves are? O Lord, take them far beyond us and use them for Your glory!

Protective Parent

As my friend and I walked, we rounded a bend and a fierce screeching pierced our ears. A mother killdeer frantically spread her wings and darted at us, noisily admonishing us to stay away from her nest in the mulch pile she guarded. We moms empathized and heeded her warning delivered in universal mom language: *"Don't mess with my kids!"*

Always Faithful

When you come to the end of all the light you know, and it's time to step into the darkness of the unknown, faith is knowing that one of two things shall happen: either you will be given something solid to stand on or you will be taught to fly.

—EDWARD TELLER

God will always come through for you, one way or another!

Jesus

The Bible paints a beautiful picture of Christ.
Did you know that He abounds in love, is
compassionate, and is our deliverer? He's also
a warrior, king, and judge who is majestic,
merciful, and mighty. He is risen, and He reigns in
righteousness. He is our savior, our shield, and our
shepherd. And the list goes on. . .and on. . .forever!

A Mother's Love

A mother's love!—how sweet the name!
The holiest, purest, tenderest flame
That kindles from above;
Within a heart of earthly mould
As much of heaven as heart can hold
Nor through eternity grows cold—
That is a mother's love.

—MONTGOMERY

No wonder our mothers' hearts feel as though they
could burst. . .God is pouring heaven into them!

Rich Kids

A rich child often sits in a poor mother's lap.

—DANISH PROVERB

No matter what your particular financial situation, if you invest your time and emotions in your children by loving them, holding them, and playing with them, your return on your investment is immeasurable. They are richer for it— and so are you.

Impressions

Children are a lot like wet cement. Whatever falls on them makes an impression.

—HAIM GINOTT

Our own inadequacies, as well as influences beyond our control, have the potential for leaving the "wrong impression" upon our children. However, the Lord desires to imprint Himself upon all of us—and His is definitely the "right impression."

Lasting Importance

A hundred years from now, it will not matter what my
bank account was, the sort of house I lived in, or the make
of car I drove. But the world may be different because I
was important in the life of a child.

—UNKNOWN

A century's passing causes unimportant things to
fade into oblivion. Motherhood is not one of them.

Future Impact

*If you plan for one year, plant rice. If you plan for ten years,
plant a tree. If you plan for one hundred years, educate a child.*

—CHINESE PROVERB

For the Christian family, education involves not only
developing the intellect, but nurturing the spirit of the
child, as well. A child who grows up to share his faith
impacts the future for Christ.

Victory!

Once during a family meal our four-year-old
declared triumphantly, "I buttered my bread!"
Unbeknownst to us, she had been laboring for
several minutes to accomplish that amazing feat.
One marvelous blessing of motherhood is observing
and celebrating the delight of a child when a lesson
is learned or a skill is accomplished—even if it's just
buttering bread!

Heart Lessons

The mother's heart is the child's schoolroom.

—HENRY WARD BEECHER

Some moments we may not want our children learning what is in our hearts! That is why we need to seek the Lord continually, allowing Him to fill us with His goodness and wisdom and perfect love. Those are the things our children need to learn.

Talk Is Cheap

There is only one way to bring up a child in the way that he should go and that is to travel that way yourself.

—ABRAHAM LINCOLN

Telling your child how he should be without living it in front of him is not only *unproductive*, but it can also be *destructive*. Let your child see that your actions agree with your words.

His Idea

When God thought of mother, He must have laughed with
satisfaction, and framed it quickly—so rich,
so deep, so divine, so full of soul, power, and beauty,
was the conception.

—HENRY WARD BEECHER

God could have designed the human race without the
necessity of mothers. But in His goodness, He chose the
family and allows us to experience the joy
of motherhood.

On Our Knees

I have been driven many times to my knees by the overwhelming conviction that I had nowhere else to go. My own wisdom, and that of all about me, seemed insufficient for the day.

—ABRAHAM LINCOLN

Family life is inherent with countless situations requiring God's wisdom. Therefore, we must pray, pray, and pray some more!

Expect the Best

The mother loves her child most divinely,
not when she surrounds him with comfort
and anticipates his wants, but when she
resolutely holds him to the highest standards
and is content with nothing less than his best.

—HAMILTON WRIGHT MABIE

Encourage your child to aspire to
godly standards and expectations—
and leave the spoiling
to Grandma!

Divine Interruptions

You are engrossed in a project and suddenly a
child clambers up on your lap with her favorite
storybook. Or you are finally enjoying some quiet
time with the Lord and your teenager chooses that
moment to be talkative. Frustrating? Sometimes.
But consider that interruptions are blessings in
disguise, and embrace them as part of what God has
for you today.

Little Things

Enjoy the little things, for one day you may look back and discover they were the big things.

—UNKNOWN

An unsolicited hug, a bouquet of tiny flowers, a "letter" to Mommy from a toddler who can't write, an "I wuv you" whispered in your ear. . .these are the little things that will become big with time's passing.

Sufficient Grace

*The will of God will not take you where
the grace of God cannot keep you.*

—UNKNOWN

It was the Lord who bestowed upon you the
distinguished title of "mother," and it is the Lord
who will supply the grace necessary to fulfill your
responsibilities in that role. His grace is sufficient.

Refreshment Served

Has speaking to the mountain done little to reduce your laundry pile? Do you feel that John 11:35, "Jesus wept," was inspired by your lack of parenting skills? Does the handwriting on the wall predict your failure as a mother? If your spirit is wilted by discouragement and your energy is sapped by defeat, ask the Lord to revive and refresh you. He is able.

Let It Shine

Love comforteth like sunshine after rain.

—WILLIAM SHAKESPEARE

How beautiful the sun appears after a soppy succession of rainy days. And how soothing and comforting is your love when expressed to your children in the wake of sadness or disappointment. Your love comforts them and brightens their days. Let it shine!

Family Fun

*There is no doubt that it is around the family and the home
that all the greatest virtues, the most dominating virtues of
human society, are created, strengthened,
and maintained.*

—WINSTON CHURCHILL

God Himself created the family in order to declare
His truth and love to the world. And maybe
also because a family is a lot of fun.

Sharing

A mother laughs our laughs,
sheds our tears,
returns our love,
fears our fears.
She lives our joys,
cares our cares
and all our hopes and dreams
she shares.

—UNKNOWN

What a lovely picture of compassionate motherhood.
Sharing our children's joy and burdens makes their
joy deeper and their burdens lighter.

Slip-Sliding

*Perhaps someday it will be pleasant
to remember even this.*

—VIRGIL

If you discover your nine-month-old
on his hands and knees sliding around
in a large puddle of cooking oil on the
kitchen floor, you have a decision to
make. You can get upset, or you can
just grab the camera, knowing that
someday the memory
will be pleasant!

It's Complimentary

If you want your children to improve, let them overhear the nice things you say about them to others.

—HAIM GINOTT

Even as adults, we like to be complimented. Others' positive opinions of us tend to encourage us to soar to greater heights and grander achievements. The same is true for our children. Let's bless them with our compliments.

Works in Progress

*Life is like playing a violin in public and learning the
instrument as one goes on.*

—SAMUEL BUTLER

The same can be said for parenting. . .you learn as you
go—and everyone is watching! Mercifully, parenting
isn't a three-strikes-and-you're-out game. Children
and parents are works in progress, and the Lord's grace
covers our growth.

Go Away

When my kids become wild and unruly, I use a nice, safe playpen. When they're finished, I climb out.

—ERMA BOMBECK

Let's face it, sometimes a mom just has to get away from the fray. Have you given yourself permission to "clock out" lately? A break is rejuvenating for your mind and body. And it might just keep you out of the playpen!

Supermom

To your family, you are a superhero. You
find what they've lost, cook what they like,
take them where they want to go, teach them
what they do not know, clean up what they
mess up, remember what they forget, share
their joys and sorrows, love them when they are
unlovable. . . . And you thought that *S* on your
cape stood for *Sleepy*.

DAY
150

Perfect Profession

"What do you want to be when you grow up?"
Children usually respond with occupations such as
a fireman or a doctor. But what if your child is called
to a very dangerous profession or one that could
take him far away from you? Your mother's heart
constricts, but the Lord can lead your child to the
perfect place—and give you peace.

Eternal Influence

*Every action of our lives touches on some
chord that will vibrate in eternity.*

—EDWIN HUBBEL CHAPIN

Your life *matters*. Like the proverbial pebble in the
pond that sends out its ripples, loving your husband,
serving your family, and sharing your faith definitely
affect eternity—yours and others' you may not even
know. Your ripples of influence are eternal!

Contagious

No act of kindness, no matter
how small, is ever wasted.

—AESOP

When, and some days *if*, I see my children
exhibiting kindness toward each other, it warms
my heart. But I also know that if they observe their
parents practicing kindness toward them and others,
they are more likely to be kind. Kindness is a great
thing for a family to spread around!

Leave It Behind

Finish each day and be done with it. You have done
what you could. Some blunders and absurdities
no doubt crept in; forget them as soon as you can.
Tomorrow is a new day; begin it well and serenely
and with too high a spirit to be encumbered with
your old nonsense.

—RALPH WALDO EMERSON

Learn from your mistakes
and move on!

DAY 154

For His Glory

Consider the talents the Lord has given you. Do you cook? Draw? Play an instrument? Sing? Design clothes? Organize? Teach? Write? Clean? God gave you your gifts and talents—even those you think don't count—to be used for His glory. When you commit them to Him, He will glorify Himself and bless you by doing amazing things through you!

Dedication

Dedicate some of your life to others. Your dedication will not be a sacrifice. It will be an exhilarating experience because it is an intense effort applied toward a meaningful end.

—DR. THOMAS DOOLEY

Sometimes it *does* feel like a sacrifice to deny your own wants to care for your family. But the Lord sees your dedication and will surely bless you for it.

True Friend

A mother is the truest friend we have, when trials, heavy and sudden, fall upon us. . .when friends, who rejoice with us in our sunshine, desert us when troubles thicken around us, still will she cling to us, and endeavor by her kind precepts and counsels to dissipate the clouds of darkness, and cause peace to return to our hearts.

—WASHINGTON IRVING

Focus

*No steam or gas drives anything until it is
confined. No life ever grows great until it is
focused, dedicated, disciplined.*

—HARRY FOSDICK

When you focus on becoming the person
the Lord intends you to be, growth in
Christ is a natural result. He can do mighty
things through a mother who is focused,
dedicated, and disciplined.

Grace

Hold yourself responsible for a higher standard than anybody else expects of you. Never excuse yourself. Never pity yourself. Be a hard master to yourself—and be lenient to everybody else.

—HENRY WARD BEECHER

Expecting more of ourselves than we do of those around us extends grace to them by accepting them the way they are. . .just the way Christ accepts us.

Perseverance

When nothing seems to help, I go and look at a
stonecutter hammering away at his rock perhaps a
hundred times without as much as a crack showing in
it. Yet at the hundred and first blow it will split in two,
and I know it was not that blow that did it—but all that
had gone before.

—JACOB RIIS

Determination

A determined soul will do more with a rusty monkey
wrench than a loafer will accomplish with all the tools in
a machine shop.

—ROBERT HUGHES

We can deluge our children with every material
possession, but if we don't teach and model
ingenuity, resourcefulness, and determination,
we end up with "lazy loafers" instead of
"determined doers."

Blessed

Her children arise and call her blessed; her husband
also, and he praises her: "Many women do noble
things, but you surpass them all."

—PROVERBS 31:28–29 NIV

Someday your family *will* bless you. . .and
maybe even thank you for all those cooking
and housecleaning lessons you are
giving them now!

Cast of Characters

I Can't *is a quitter,* I Don't Know *is lazy,* I Wish I
Could *is a wisher,* I Might *is waking up,* I Will Try *is
on his feet,* I Can *is on his way,* I Will *is at work,* I Did *is
now the boss.*

—EARL CASSEL

Let's take our children from "I can't" to "I did!"

Prayer

*Trouble and perplexity drive me to prayer, and prayer drives
away perplexity and trouble.*

—PHILIPP MELANCHTHON

Synonyms for "trouble" are difficulty, dilemma, and
problem. "Perplexity" means bewilderment, bafflement,
and confusion. How many of these have you
experienced just today? Let prayer drive them away.

A Morning Resolve

I will this day try to live a simple, sincere, and serene life; repelling promptly every thought of discontent, anxiety, discouragement, impurity, and self-seeking; cultivating cheerfulness, magnanimity, charity, and the habit of holy silence; exercising economy in expenditure, carefulness in conversation, diligence in appointed service, fidelity to every trust, and a childlike trust in God.

—JOHN H. VINCENT

Partners in Parenting

Patience is the companion of wisdom.

—ST. AUGUSTINE

Another word for companion is "escort."
Picture walking through life escorted
by patience on one side and wisdom on
the other. What does one have to do with
the other? It is wise to exercise patience,
and patience is necessary to acquire
wisdom. Make them both
lifelong partners!

Cultivating Kids

Raising children is like growing a garden. You strive
to keep the weeds from choking out the desired
plants. You also must recognize the specific needs
of each variety of plant and remember to feed
and water them so they won't wilt. But the main
similarity is that with loads of love, care, prayer, and
hard labor, you can achieve beautiful results!

God's Gift

*You don't choose your family. They are God's gift to you,
as you are to them.*

—DESMOND TUTU

How remarkable that God Himself assembles our
families! When we allow Him to work not just in the
"assembly stage" but throughout our lives,
His reasons for putting us together "just so" will
become increasingly apparent. And we will
reap the blessings of His work.

DAY
168

Trustworthy

> All I have seen teaches me to trust
> the Creator for all I have not seen.

—RALPH WALDO EMERSON

God's creation gloriously declares His existence and goodness with beauty and majesty. Even the very sight of our children should ignite in us such an awe of our great God that we trust Him implicitly with the unseen. He is worthy of our trust.

Fair and Honest

*Live so that when your children think of fairness
and integrity, they think of you.*

—H. JACKSON BROWN JR.

Be as fair as possible within the realistic
limitations of this life that is not fair.
And demonstrate such a high level of
integrity (honesty, truthfulness, reliability)
that your children trust you
completely and desire to be
trustworthy themselves.

Positive Kids

*When you put faith, hope, and love together,
you can raise positive kids in a negative world.*

—ZIG ZIGLAR

Our faith is in Christ who overcame the ultimate
negative—death—and turned it into a positive—
life. Because of that faith we have hope, and we are
loved with an everlasting love. Faith, hope, and love:
the eternally effective antidote to negativity.

Parenting on Purpose

*Children are not casual guests in our home.
They have been loaned to us temporarily for the
purpose of loving them and instilling a foundation
of values on which their future lives will be built.*

—JAMES C. DOBSON

This speaks of purposeful parenting whereby we
impart to our children values that will serve them well
throughout their lives. And eternity.

Day 172

Good Influence

We like to think it is enough if we keep our own lives straight. Quite plainly it is not. If we talk cynically or encourage a lowering of standards, even though we still control our own actions, we become responsible for the failure of those who, weakened by our influence, fail to stand upright.

—GEORGE P.T. SARGENT

A mother wields a powerful influence!

Think Kindness

God is even kinder than you think.

—ST. TERESA

Today is a good day for you and your
family to contemplate the kindness of
God. No matter how much kindness you
attribute to Him, He possesses even more.
You can never really comprehend how
kind God is because He doesn't *have* an
amount of kindness—He
just *is* kindness.

Lovely Touch

*God's fingers can touch nothing
but to mold it into loveliness.*

—GEORGE MACDONALD

God, by His very nature, is simply incapable
of performing any act or speaking any word or
thinking any thought that does not emanate
loveliness and beauty. Just as in God there is no
darkness, no mistruth, no evil, there likewise is no
ugliness. His touch fashions only loveliness.

Let Go

Anxiety usually comes from strain, and strain is caused by too complete a dependence on ourselves, on our own devices, our own plans, our own idea of what we are able to do.

THOMAS MERTON

The more schedules I create and the more control I attempt to wield, the greater my anxiety level and the less I accomplish. Lord, help me *let go*.

Things Worth Remembering

The value of time,
The success of perseverance,
The pleasure of working,
The dignity of simplicity,
The worth of character,
The improvement of talent,
The influence of example,
The obligation of duty,
The wisdom of economy,
The virtue of patience,
The joy of originating,
The power of kindness.

—UNKNOWN

Spread Joy

*A happy, joyful spirit spreads joy everywhere;
a fretful spirit is a trouble to ourselves
and to all around us.*

—UNKNOWN

Sometimes it can burden us with a
considerable amount of pressure,
but we moms generally do set the tone in
our homes. If we are feeling fretful,
we need to count our blessings
with a grateful spirit
and spread joy.

Content

Those who face that which is actually before them,
unburdened by the past, undistracted by the future, these
are they who live, who make the best use of their lives;
these are those who have found the secret of contentment.

—ALBAN GOODIER

The Lord is able to remove our burdens, past and
future, and help us to be content with our present.

Daily Surrender

*Relying on God has to begin all over again every day
as if nothing had yet been done.*

—C. S. LEWIS

This speaks of such dependence on God that we
start each day by surrendering every detail, even the
things we gave up yesterday. Daily surrender equals
daily peace. And daily peace will ultimately become a
lifetime of peace.

Freedom

Happiness is more than anything that serene, secure, happy freedom from guilt.

—HENRIK IBSEN

Usually a mom can find something to feel guilty about, whether or not it is valid. "Did I play with them enough? Did I fix healthy food? Was I too harsh? Was I strict enough?" We must learn to listen only to the Lord's conviction and throw out the guilt.

Always More

*Now glory be to God! By his mighty
power at work within us, he is able to
accomplish infinitely more than we
would ever dare to ask or hope*

—EPHESIANS 3:20 NLT

Ask for the impossible and hope for the
unimaginable and God is able to do *more*.
You cannot out-dream God!

Remember the Blessings

Always remember to forget,
the troubles that passed away.
But never forget to remember,
the blessings that come each day.

—IRISH BLESSING

Dwelling on your blessings is the best way *not* to dwell on your troubles. Engage your mind so fully with thoughts of God's continual blessings that no thinking space remains to squander on past difficulties.

Anchor Chain

*Never forget the three powerful resources you always have
available to you: love, prayer, and forgiveness.*

—H. JACKSON BROWN JR.

Think of these as links in the anchor chain that holds
your ship steady. They are tightly interconnected: love
calls us to prayer, and prayer is the means by which we
can extend forgiveness. They make a strong
chain indeed.

Day 184

Teaching the Future

Where will our country find leaders with integrity, courage, strength—all the family values—in ten, twenty, or thirty years? The answer is that you are teaching them, loving them, and raising them right now.

—BARBARA BUSH

Your children who are learning life truths today are tomorrow's adults who will teach and lead others to those truths.

The Real You

Let's talk about you for a minute. I mean just *you*—not mom, wife, sister, friend, or daughter. Of course, a large part of who you are is shaped by all the different roles you assume. But I hope you haven't forgotten that you are an eternally valuable person apart from all your responsibilities and titles. God loves YOU. Period.

Secret Hope

Oliver Wendell Holmes stated, "Youth fades, love droops, the leaves of friendship fall; a mother's secret hope outlives them all." Apart from dreaming of him cleaning his room, what is your secret hope for your child? Or better yet, what is God's? Pray, believe, and watch it transpire.

Weather Forecast

Conflict in a family is like the weather: *you will have some*. When, how much, and what kind are the questions. You might go several days with no cloud in sight, then a storm builds and you are deluged with a surge of bickering or a cold spell of aloofness. And then, blessedly, the sunny skies and warm breezes return. *Ahh...*

Handle with Care

Peace is not absence of conflict; it is the ability to handle conflict by peaceful means.

—RONALD REAGAN

You can enjoy a peaceful home even though you experience conflict. If controversies are handled wisely and justly with the Lord's help, the general undertone of peace remains because a family whose peace comes from the Lord won't be overly shaken by conflict.

Power of Words

*A word once let out of the cage
cannot be whistled back again.*

—HORACE

We must teach our children the biblical
principle of the power of the tongue. The child's
verse about sticks and stones is simply not
true—words *can* hurt. But they also hold
the power to bring joy and healing
when chosen with love
and consideration
of others.

Great Enough

*I have a great need for Christ; I have a great
Christ for my need.*

—CHARLES SPURGEON

There is absolutely no need so great that He cannot
meet it. There is no problem so huge that He cannot
solve it. There is no child so impossible that He
cannot discipline him. And there is no mother so
exhausted that He cannot revive her.

Contentment

Our natural inclination is to compare ourselves and our
children to others. "Are mine as smart as hers?
Are mine as well behaved as hers? Am I as good a
mom as she is?" But comparison is the enemy of
contentment. To be content means to be satisfied with
what you have, and we are satisfied when we are happy
with God's provision.

Healthy Home

The family should be a closely knit group. The home should be a self-contained shelter of security; a kind of school where life's basic lessons are taught; and a kind of church where God is honored; a place where wholesome recreation and simple pleasures are enjoyed.

—BILLY GRAHAM

Goodnight Kisses

*Always kiss your children goodnight,
even if they're already asleep.*

—H. JACKSON BROWN JR.

No mother really needs to be told this. Most
likely you already sneak in to your child's
room, brush a tender kiss on her sweet
forehead, gaze at her in the dim light,
and wonder when it happened
that someone left a larger child
in her place....

Preacher Moms

I learned more about Christianity from my mother than from all the theologians in England.

—JOHN WESLEY

As mothers, we preach a thousand sermons a day to our kids, not only through our words but by our actions, as well. What message will they receive from us? Let it be one of Christlike love, humility, joy, and commitment—a sermon worth remembering.

Balancing Act

Imagine an airplane struggling to get airborne
with a ton of cargo strapped to one wing, or a
gymnast attempting to balance on a beam holding
an anvil on one arm, or driving a car whose tires are
out of balance. Balance is critical in many areas, but
especially in our personal lives. Let's balance our
work, play, rest, and worship.

Special Creation

*The woman who makes a sweet, beautiful home,
filling it with love and prayer and purity, is doing
something better than anything else her hands
could find to do beneath the skies.*

—J. R. MILLER

Sure, there are many noble vocations, honorable
careers, and worthy pursuits, but a loving and godly
mother is a unique and highly valued creation
of God.

No Worries

Worry is faith in the negative; trust in
the unpleasant; assurance of disaster and
belief in defeat. Worry is wasting today's time
to clutter up tomorrow's opportunities with
yesterday's troubles.

—UNKNOWN

If you looked up "mother" in a thesaurus,
would "worry" be listed as a synonym?
Let's edit our entry to include
"faith" and stop worrying!

Too Good

An ideal Christian home ought to be a place where love rules. It ought to be beautiful, bright, joyous, full of tenderness and affection, a place in which all are growing happier and holier each day.

—J. R. MILLER

Sounds too good to be true except that our God *is* able to transform our homes and hearts and make us "happier and holier each day."

DAY
199

Power Provision

For men have no taste for [God's power] till they are convinced of their need of it and they immediately forget its value unless they are conditionally reminded by awareness of their own weakness.

—JOHN CALVIN

Mothering requires an admission of weakness, a declaration of "Help! I can't do this on my own!" That is the moment of God's great provision of power.

DAY
200

Passionate Parenting

*God loves with a great love the man whose heart is
bursting with a passion for the impossible.*

—WILLIAM BOOTH

If there is anything that appears to be impossible,
it is motherhood. And no doubt your heart is
passionate about it to the point of bursting. God
loves and honors your passionate heart and
transforms your impossibilities into realities.

New Clothes

*It is God who arms me with strength
and makes my way perfect.*

—PSALM 18:32 NIV

The original Hebrew of this verse paints a
more vivid picture of what God does for you:
He *clothes* you with *might* and *efficiency*
and makes your *journey complete*! His
clothes will fit you perfectly!

Conflict Resolution

When conflict arises, it is imperative that we take the time to see it resolved. If it is allowed to boil and fester, bitterness and anger will take root in our hearts and homes. With the Lord's strength and discernment, though, we can work through conflict and uproot bitterness. Then plant love, understanding, and forgiveness in its place.

Treasure Map

*Where your pleasure is, there is your treasure; where your
treasure is, there is your heart; where your heart is,
there is your happiness.*

—ST. AUGUSTINE

If we trace a path from our happiness, we find our
hearts. If we trace the path from our hearts, it leads
to our ultimate treasure—faith in Christ. And our
beautiful families are extra pleasures from His hand.

DAY
204

All We Need

In Christ we have a love that can never be fathomed; a life that can never die; a righteousness that can never be tarnished; a peace that can never be understood; a rest that can never be disturbed; a joy that can never be diminished; a hope that can never be disappointed. . .and resources that can never be exhausted.

—UNKNOWN

Discipline Required

Children need to learn how to do things which they do not want to do, when those things ought to be done. Older people have to do a great many things from a sense of duty. Unless children are trained to recognize duty as more binding than inclination, they will suffer all their lives through from their lack of discipline.

—H. CLAY TRUMBULL

Prayer Mercies

*What a mercy was it to us to have parents that prayed for
us before they had us, as well as in our infancy when we
could not pray for ourselves!*

—JOHN FLAVEL

Even if you didn't have praying parents, you can
alter the pattern and transform future generations
by praying for your family—present and future.
What mercies they will see!

Sure Thing

Do you find it difficult not to second-guess yourself
on parenting decisions? Do you overanalyze every
judgment you make and end up more confused? Be
encouraged by the fact that your concern for making
the right decision indicates that you truly want to "get it
right." Seek wisdom and confidence from the Lord, and
He will help you be decisive and sure.

God Appreciates You

Only God Himself fully appreciates the influence of a Christian mother in the molding of character in her children.

—BILLY GRAHAM

Remember this when you experience those moments of feeling unappreciated. The Lord truly understands the complexities and difficulties inherent in shaping your children's character. And He values your dedication to the task.

Rest!

Rest time is not waste time. It is economy to gather fresh strength. . . . It is wisdom to take occasional furlough. In the long run, we shall do more by sometimes doing less.

—CHARLES SPURGEON

The Lord doesn't expect mothers to work themselves to death, even though the workload makes the prospect appear likely. We simply must take time to rest!

Endurance

He conquers who endures.

—UNKNOWN

This saying could be attributed to any of the
millions of conquering mothers who are
determined to see the bottom of their laundry
baskets, the last dirty dish washed and put away,
the last bath given at night, and the time when she
will lay down her weary head and her sleeping baby
does not instantly awaken.

Soft Advice

*Advice is like snow; the softer it falls, the longer it dwells upon,
and the deeper it sinks into the mind.*

SAMUEL TAYLOR COLERIDGE

As your children mature and desire more
independence, it is wise to let your advice fall softly
upon them. Conversing with them lightheartedly while
gently sharing your opinion is more effective than
verbally pounding it home.

Mouths of Babes

We were getting ready for Bible study when I told my two-year-old where her shoes were. Happy to locate them, she plopped down to put them on, looked up at me, smiled sweetly, and declared, "You good mom!" I treasured her comment and desire for you to do the same because I know it's also true for you. You good mom!

Morning Prayer

Lord, thank You that I am alive. Thank You
for Your mercies that are new every morning.
Thank You for the privilege of being called
"Mom." Thank You that while I was sleeping,
You were busy working on my behalf. Thank
You for my husband and each of our children.
I trust You to meet our needs in mighty ways
today and every day. Amen.

Sweet Sleep

*There may be those on earth who dress better or eat better,
but those who enjoy the peace of God sleep better.*

—L. THOMAS HOLDCROFT

Moms are notorious for operating on less sleep
than humanly required, but when you do actually
sleep, God's peace ensures your sleep will be sweet.
And sweet sleep is infinitely more valuable than
expensive clothes and fine food!

Listen to Advice

How do you feel when a friend attempts to give you
instruction or advice? Defensive? Offended? Hurt? Or
do you readily accept the instruction in the spirit it is
given? Sure, it is wise to measure it against God's word
to determine its validity. If it measures up, keep it; and if
not, discard it. But *listen*.

Home

A house is built of logs and stone,
Of tiles and posts and piers;
A home is built of loving deeds
That stand a thousand years.

—VICTOR HUGO

A person can build a house, but without a loving family in it, it is just an empty shell. Fill it with a family that lives, laughs, and loves together, and it becomes a home.

Laugh!

I *hasten to laugh at everything, for
fear of being obliged to weep.*

—PIERRE BEAUMARCHAIS

When a preschooler smeared diaper cream all
over his toy fire engine, he explained to his
exasperated mom, "It was a little bit red!"
A child's antics can be harmless in the long
run but cause us hassle now. We can
choose to laugh or cry. Let's go
for laughter.

Sacred Calling

*God sends many beautiful things to this world, many
noble gifts; but no blessing is richer than that which
He bestows in a mother who has learned love's lessons
well, and has realized something of the
meaning of her sacred calling.*

—J. R. MILLER

When you realize that motherhood is indeed a
sacred calling, your perspective is forever changed
from the temporal to the eternal.

Continual Chance

In His graciousness, the Lord gives you a new chance
every minute of every hour of every day to grow and
become the person He desires you to be. You will never
hear Him say, "That was your last chance! I've had it
with you!" Some say He is the God of second chances.
He's actually the God of the *continual* chance.
It's called grace.

Just Trust

Let us trust God where we cannot trace Him.

—CHARLES SPURGEON

Wouldn't it be nice if God provided a schematic of exactly how He's working, what He's going to do and when? Sometimes His workings are clearly seen, but other times, we cannot trace His hand. Those are the times our trust is tested most. But that is the essence of faith.

GPS

My GPS directed me down a wrong road then
instructed, "When possible, make a U-turn."
Fortunately, God—the perfect Parent—has no
software glitches that will lead you the wrong
way. Psalm 32:8 promises, "I will instruct you
and teach you in the way you should go; I will
guide you with My eye" (NKJV). Call it *God's
Parenting System*.

Savor the Moments

Moms are busy people. We have demands pulling at us from every direction while we are running in every direction. Even in our busyness, though, we need to savor the moments the Lord gives us with our children, to focus on each moment, rather than looking ahead to the next. Right now is the only moment we can truly hold on to.

Speak Their Language

Children desperately need to know—and to hear in ways they understand and remember—that they're loved and valued by mom and dad.

—PAUL SMALLY

Children come with all different personalities. You may have a hugger and a non-hugger or a verbal child and a nonverbal child. Whatever the case, speak your love to them in their individual language.

Nobody's Perfect

Say this with me: *There is no perfect mother.* There now, don't you feel better? No matter how it appears, no matter how perfect someone looks, no one gets this motherhood thing exactly right all the time. We are all works in progress who make mistakes—sometimes big ones. Good thing our goal isn't to be perfect. It's to be perfectly usable.

Different Is Good

Oh, it's tempting to compare ourselves with others. But that's like analyzing bananas to determine what apples should look like. You see, we are all *different* people on a *different* journey encountering *different* obstacles, learning *different* lessons, and *mothering different children*. But we serve the same Lord who doesn't compare us to each other but instead delights in our differences.

Creative God

Serving a creative God comes in handy when
you are in a parenting predicament. For instance,
you have two children whose genders and age
differences combine (or *combust*) to create an
atmosphere of constant quarreling. God can give
you creative means to resolve the conflict between
them. I really know He can. That's why I'm waiting
so patiently. . . .

Delighted

The Lord delights in a godly mother who desires above
all to teach her children about Him and who lives her
faith in front of them daily. He delights in a mother
who faithfully goes about her tasks with a spirit of
thankfulness and gratefulness. And He delights in a
mother whose joy permeates all of her relationships
because she delights in Him.

Nobody Told You

When you signed up for this race called
motherhood, did they tell you it's a marathon of vast
distance and that the track is covered with hurdles?
That it's a survival exercise with wild beasts to
subdue, train, and feed? That it's like skiing down a
snow-packed slope at breakneck speed while reading
a book about skiing? I thought not.

Faith

Faith upholds a Christian under all trials by assuring him that every painful dispensation is under the direction of his Lord; that chastisements are a token of His love; that the season, measure, and continuance of his sufferings are appointed by Infinite Wisdom, and designed to work for his everlasting good; and that grace and strength shall be afforded him, according to his need.

—JOHN NEWTON

True Promises

God has not promised skies always blue, flower-strewn pathways all our life through; God has not promised sun without rain, joy without sorrow, peace without pain. But God has promised strength for the day, rest for the labor, light for the way; grace for the trials, help from above, unfailing sympathy, undying love.

—UNKNOWN

Knowing God

*We never become truly spiritual by sitting
down and wishing to be so.*

—PHILLIPS BROOKS

Anyone who desires to know God must make a
concerted effort to know Him. Praying, reading His
Word, listening to Him speak to our hearts. . .those are
the means by which we come to know Him. And if we
know Him, we can lead our children to Him.

Attitude

We don't like it when our kids have bad attitudes. We admonish them to change their attitudes, to straighten up, to act right. But I wonder if the Lord isn't trying to tell us the same things. Maybe He would like our attitudes to reflect the miracle of life and forgiveness He has given us, and transform our children's attitudes in the process.

Perspective

When a mother saw a thunderstorm forming in mid-afternoon, she worried about her seven-year-old daughter who would be walking the three blocks from school to home. Deciding to meet her, the mother saw her walking nonchalantly along, stopping to smile whenever lightning flashed. Seeing her mother, the little girl ran to her, explaining happily, "All the way home, God's been taking my picture!"

—UNKNOWN

Continual Surrender

The giving of self to the service of God is not like making a single offer, handing over a single gift, receiving a single acknowledgment. It is a continued action, renewed all the time.

—HUBERT VAN ZELLER

There is a certain peace in daily surrender. Before your feet land on the floor in the morning, give God your day.

Serenity

In Jesus there is the quiet, strong serenity of one who seeks to conquer by love, and not by strife of words.

—WILLIAM BARCLAY

If you struggle with frustrations that cause
you to speak to your children in a spirit of strife,
you are not alone. But know that the more serenity
we draw from Christ, the better we will learn to
communicate calmly and appropriately.

Heart and Mind

*Scientists are attempting to come to God headfirst. They
must come to Him heart-first. Then let their heads
interpret what they have found.*

—HENRY WARD BEECHER

Feed your child's heart with the beautiful and
matchless character of God, and immerse his mind
in the truths of God. Then his mind and heart
cannot help but agree with each other.

Single Mom?

Perhaps you are a single mother and the readings in this book that mention husbands are difficult for you. If so, I pray you have found encouragement anyway, and understand that you are valued and loved by God. If you are married, I encourage you to pray for single mothers as they faithfully and courageously fulfill their responsibilities to their children.

God's Strength

The whole trouble is that we won't let God help us.

—GEORGE MACDONALD

Overwhelmed? Exhausted? Frustrated?
Understandable. But it's not what God desires
for you. He wants to lift your burdens and show
Himself strong. If you have the willingness and
faithfulness to do, God will provide the strength.
Remember, when we are weak, we are strong.

Patience

*Patience is not passive; on the contrary,
it is active; it is concentrated strength.*

—ANONYMOUS

Let's not confuse patience with passiveness or lack of
concern, a sort of "whatever will be, will be" philosophy.
In the Bible, patience is equated with endurance and
perseverance, both of which speak of strength. When
you are patient, you are strong!

Love Letter

I am a little pencil in the hand of a writing God who is sending a love letter to the world.

—MOTHER TERESA

As mothers, we are the pencils with which God writes His love on our children's hearts. When they become parents, He will continue writing His love letter through them.

Press On

I press on toward the goal to win the
*prize for which God has called me
heavenward in Christ Jesus.*

—PHILIPPIANS 3:14 NIV

The dishes will fill the sink again,
Laundry Mountain will erupt again, and
the kids will misbehave again. On and on
it goes…but so do God's eternal promises
when you press on!

Listen

Give us grace to listen well.

—JOHN KEBLE

Our ears may hear people speaking to us, but do we listen with our minds and hearts? Many times I have heard from my children, "Are you listening to me?" They aren't asking if the sound waves sufficiently vibrated my eardrums. They want to know if I cared enough to *listen*—and not just with my ears.

Mothering

My body is tired
My mind is mired
It has become distressing.
But just when I think
I'm on the brink
God gives me another blessing.
Hugs and a kiss
Heavenly bliss
Upon me He's impressing
A child's love
Is far above
Others worth possessing.

First Step

*Faith is taking the first step even when you
don't see the whole staircase.*

—MARTIN LUTHER KING JR.

This line takes on a more literal meaning if one has
teenagers whose bedrooms are upstairs, and their
folded laundry languishes on the stairs waiting to be
put away. Rarely do we see the "whole staircase." But
we take that first step anyway. . . .

Small Joys

*The happiness of life is made up of
minute fractions—the little, soon forgotten
charities of a kiss or a smile, a kind
look or heartfelt compliment.*

—SAMUEL TAYLOR COLERIDGE

Enjoying a sticky kiss from a toddler,
witnessing a baby's first smile, observing your
teenager's pleasant countenance, or
receiving a sincere compliment from
your child. . .those are the small joys
that make life happy.

Taught by Trials

A smooth sea never made a skillful mariner.

—ENGLISH PROVERB

Navigating the waters of parenthood is challenging,
especially when the waters are stirred up by trials
and conflict. But in those times, we acquire a
greater depth of wisdom and insight from the Lord,
which will enable us to manage the next storm
effectively—and have peace in the midst of it.

Choices

Moms are faced with many choices throughout each day. From deciding what to cook for dinner or how to handle particular situations with our children, we make numerous decisions on a daily basis. But in the many things that happen about which we have no choice, we can only choose how we respond. Let it be in faith and trust.

DAY 248

Cherished

Children will not remember you for the material things you provided but for the feeling that you cherished them.

—RICHARD L. EVANS

The assurance of being cherished will greatly outlast a tricycle or a computer or expensive clothes. A hug, a compliment, a smile, a special favor—all these assure your child she is cherished.

What?

"I'm counting to three and I'm on two. . .one, two, three!" Upon hearing this ridiculous declaration, the kids burst out laughing, and their suspicion that my mental agility was, uh, *slipping*, was confirmed. My response? I laughed with them and it diffused the tension. Not a bad thing!

A God Thing

We find a delight in the beauty and happiness of children that makes the heart too big for the body.

—RALPH WALDO EMERSON

Children do bring such beauty and happiness into our lives, at times it seems our hearts cannot contain it. How can it be that small humans with such high maintenance requirements bring such joy? It's a God thing.

Committed to Contentment

Christian contentment is that sweet,
inward, quiet, gracious frame of spirit,
which freely submits to and delights in God's
wise and fatherly disposal in every condition.

—JEREMIAH BURROUGHS

Believing that He truly will do what's best for you,
knowing that He is in control. . .that's contentment. Be
committed to being content with God's provision.

God Is Already There

The next moment is as much beyond our grasp, and as much in God's care, as that a hundred years away. Care for the next minute is as foolish as care for a day in the next thousand years. In neither can we do anything, in both God is doing everything.

—C. S. LEWIS

This Day

This is the beginning of a new day. God has given me this day to use. . . . When tomorrow comes, this day will be gone forever, leaving in its place something that I have traded for it. I want it to be gain, not loss; good, not evil; success, not failure; in order that I shall not regret the price I paid for it.

—UNKNOWN

Certain Love

*Be absolutely certain that our Lord loves you, devotedly
and individually, loves you just as you are. . . .
Accustom yourself to the wonderful thought that
God loves you with a tenderness, a generosity,
and an intimacy that surpasses all your dreams.*

—ABBE HENRI DE TOURVILLE

Of all the uncertainties in this life, God's love is not
one of them.

Never Again

Dinosaurs in my bathtub
Building blocks on the floor
Stuffed animals in my bed
Handprints on the door.

Peanut butter, jelly kisses
Macaroni and cheese
Picture books and bedtime prayers
Memories are made of these.

Homework, college tests
Career decisions then
Suddenly my child is grown—
Never small again.

Only on the Lord

When you have no helpers, see all your helpers in God. When you have many helpers, see God in all your helpers. When you have nothing but God, see all in God; when you have everything, see God in everything. Under all conditions, stay thy heart only on the Lord.

—CHARLES SPURGEON

Make It So

May God give us a pure heart so we may see
Him; a humble heart so we may hear
Him; a loving heart so we may serve
Him; a faithful heart so we may live Him.

—DAG HAMMARSKJOLD

Oh, to have a pure, humble, loving,
and faithful heart! And to see, hear,
serve, and *live* Him. Make it so, Lord.

In His Hand

Hidden in the hollow
Of His blessed hand,
Never foe can follow,
Never traitor stand;
Not a surge of worry,
Not a shade of care,
Not a blast of hurry
Touch the Spirit there.

—FRANCES RIDLEY HAVERGAL

You are safe in the "hollow of His blessed hand." He protects you, removes your worries and cares, and gives you peace.

He Loves You

Perhaps you picked up this book today because you need encouragement to endure and assurance of the Lord's presence in the pandemonium. Maybe this is a day when "mother" means "malicious" and "kid" is equal to "cantankerous." If so, know that God understands where you are emotionally, spiritually, and physically this moment. *He loves you.* And His love transcends your circumstances.

DAY 260

God's Bouquet

The splendor of the rose and the whiteness of the lily do not rob the little violet of its scent nor the daisy of its simple charm. If every tiny flower wanted to be a rose, spring would lose its loveliness.

—THÉRÈSE OF LISIEUX

Each person in your home was especially created by God, and together you all comprise a unique and beautiful bouquet.

Praise the Lord

Let the word of Christ dwell in you
richly as you teach and admonish one
another with all wisdom, and as you sing
psalms, hymns and spiritual songs with
gratitude in your hearts to God.

—COLOSSIANS 3:16 NIV

What better activity than to study and
praise the Lord together!

Immeasurable Love

No created being can ever know how much and how
sweetly and tenderly God loves them. It is only with the
help of His grace that we are able to persevere. . .with
endless wonder at His high, surpassing,
immeasurable love.

—JULIAN OF NORWICH

Let your perseverance be fueled by the continual
challenge of comprehending His love. You keep
going while He keeps loving.

Never Alone

You are infinitely dear to the Father, unspeakably precious to Him. You are never, not for one second, alone.

—NORMAN F. DOWTY

If you have small children at home, that phrase "never alone" is probably not a positive! But just for a moment, reflect on the fact that God never, ever leaves you. He sticks even closer to you than your toddler.

Extraordinary Work

*Ordinary work, which is what most of us do most of the
time, is ordained by God every bit as much as
is the extraordinary.*

—ELISABETH ELLIOT

Dishes, laundry, bathroom cleaning, diaper
changing, meal preparation, vacuuming. . .those
are pretty ordinary activities. But to God, they are
extraordinary when they are performed in His name
for His purposes.

Peace

Peace with God brings peace of God.
It is a peace that settles our nerves, fills our mind,
floods our spirit, and in the midst of the uproar
around us, gives us the assurance that everything is
all right

—BOB MUMFORD

Are you in the midst of uproar? Allow
God's peace to settle your nerves because
in Him, everything *is* all right.

Get Ready!

When God is about to do something great, He starts with
a difficulty. When He is about to do something truly
magnificent, He starts with an impossibility.

—ARMIN GESSWEIN

Wow, we must really be in for something great
and magnificent because we face difficulties and
impossibilities almost daily. Bring it on, Lord!

Christian in the House

A wise person truly said, "It ought to be as impossible to
forget that there is a Christian in the house as it
s to forget that there is a ten-year-old boy in it."

—ROGER J SQUIRE

Just as a young boy makes his presence in the house
known, so should the professing Christian.
Perhaps more quietly, though.

The Expert

When I bragged to my mechanically inclined husband that my new mixer has 575 horsepower, he informed me (while choking back laughter) that it actually has 575 *watts*. The difference in our respective levels of pertinent knowledge was evident: he knew the subject. I didn't. It's the same way with God. He knows, and I don't. That makes Him the expert!

Impossible

*Start by doing what's necessary; then
do what's possible; and suddenly you are doing
the impossible.*

—ST. FRANCIS OF ASSISI

Getting out of bed in the morning is
necessary. Grabbing a shower before the
kids wake up is teetering on the outer edge
of possible. Preparing meals, refereeing
fights, cleaning house, running errands,
staying awake all day? Impossible.
But Mama, you still do it!

Day 270

A Prayer

Give me, O Lord, a steadfast heart which no unworthy
thought can drag downwards; an unconquered heart
which no tribulation can wear out; an upright heart
which no unworthy purpose may tempt aside. Bestow
upon me also. . .understanding to know You, diligence
to seek You, wisdom to find You, and a faithfulness
that may finally embrace You; through Jesus Christ,
our Lord.

—THOMAS AQUINAS

Best Gifts

The best gifts to give:
To your friend, loyalty;
To your enemy, forgiveness;
To your boss, service;
To a child, a good example;
To your parents, gratitude and devotion;
To your mate, love and faithfulness;
To all men and women, charity.

—OREN ARNOLD

The best gifts we give our children are not
wrapped in tinsel and tissue.

DAY
272

Whole Heart

*Speak tenderly to them. Let there be kindness in your face,
in your eyes, in your smile, in the warmth of your greeting.
Always have a cheerful smile. Don't only give your care,
but give your heart as well.*

—J. S. BACH

Let your speech and your countenance show that
you love with your whole heart.

Blessings

In much the same way we bless our Lord when we, as His children, honor and obey Him, He desires to bless us through our children. We are blessed by their love most assuredly, but also by their honor and obedience. If we teach them these character traits, we will surely be blessed.

Day
274

Encourager

*Christians are like the several flowers in a garden
that have each of them the dew of heaven,
which, being shaken with the wind, they let fall at
each other's roots, whereby they are jointly nourished,
and become nourishers of each other.*

—JOHN BUNYAN

Share some of the encouragement you have
received with another mom. She will soak it up
like dew.

He Keeps You

Let your faith in Christ be in the quiet confidence
that He will every day and every moment keep you
as the apple of His eye, keep you in perfect peace and
in the sure experience of all the light and the
strength you need.

—ANDREW MURRAY

DAY
276

Powerful God

The God who orchestrates the universe has a good many
things to consider that have not occurred to me, and it is
well that I leave them to Him.

—ELISABETH ELLIOT

God is omniscient and omnipotent, so He knows
everything about your family—and every other
family in the world—and will work according to
that knowledge. He has the power.

Priorities

*When we learn to say a deep, passionate
yes to the things that really matter. . .then
peace begins to settle onto our lives like
golden sunlight sifting to a forest floor.*

—THOMAS KINKADE

Obviously, you have said "yes" to motherhood,
and motherhood definitely matters to the
Lord. When our priorities agree with His,
we have peace.

Big God

*Why do so many Christians pray such tiny prayers
when their God is so big?*

—WATCHMAN NEE

Sometimes it's not the amount of praying we do
but the amount we are asking God to do that's the
problem. We need to let God out of our box, set
much higher expectations, and show our children
just how big our God really is!

He Gives

We can walk without fear, full of hope and courage and strength to do His will, waiting for the endless good which He is always giving as fast as He can get us able to take it in.

—GEORGE MACDONALD

Mothering truly feels like God is "giving as fast as He can." Sometimes it's blessings, sometimes it's lessons, but it's always good.

On His Heart

It is but right that our hearts should be on God, when the heart of God is so much on us.

—RICHARD BAXTER

Imagine that the God of the universe concerns Himself with you. Every moment, every day, always, His eye is on you and your family because you are dear to His heart. Seems fair that He be dear to yours.

Hope in Him

This I recall to my mind, therefore I have hope. Through the LORD's mercies we are not consumed, because His compassions fail not. They are new every morning; great is Your faithfulness. "The LORD is my portion," says my soul, "therefore I hope in Him!"

—LAMENTATIONS 3:21–24 NKJV

Choose Joy

Joy does not simply happen to us. We have to choose joy and keep choosing it every day.

—HENRI NOUWEN

A few years back, I decided to leave up one Christmas decoration year-round. The silver block letters sit on our mantle to remind me of what I can choose each day: J-O-Y.

Sunshine

*Those who bring sunshine into the lives of others,
cannot keep it from themselves.*

—J. M. BARRIE

When you shine your light of joy upon those around
you, some of that radiance is sure to reflect back to you.
If a simple "I love you" spoken to your child prompts
him to say it back, you are treated to a ray of sunshine.

Good Mother

*There's no way to be a perfect mother, and a
million ways to be a good one.*

—JILL CHURCHILL

Rule out perfection and focus on blessing your
children. Whether it is by surprising them with a
special gift, preparing their favorite meal, or even
disciplining them, you are blessing them in love.
And love negates the need for perfection.

Lessons for Life

While we try to teach our children all
about life, our children teach us what
life is all about.

ANGELA SCHWINDT

We teach our children responsibility,
compassion, self-sacrifice, forgiveness, and
God's love. And through teaching them,
we learn responsibility, compassion, self-
sacrifice, forgiveness, and God's love.
Think God planned it that way?

Heart Treasure

Oh, the little arms that encircle
My neck in their tender embrace
Oh, the smiles that are halos of heaven,
Shedding sunshine of love on my face.

—CHARLES M. DICKINSON

If only we could seal up those hugs and smiles in
our hearts, that time would not erase them. . .

Always Loving

*The great love of God is an ocean
without a bottom or a shore.*

CHARLES SPURGEON

Even greater than your sea of laundry and your expanse
of never-ending housework, His love is bottomless
and boundless. You can never reach the outer edge, nor
can you exhaust the supply. God absolutely never stops
loving because He cannot cease being Himself.

Hope in God

Hope does not necessarily take the form of excessive
confidence; rather, it involves the simple
willingness to take the next step.

—STANLEY HAUERWAS

Hope and confidence can only be found in the Lord.
Because we hope in Him, we can take a step with
confidence, trusting that He will show us the
next one.

Peace and Quiet

A quiet morning with a loving God puts the events of the upcoming day into proper perspective.

—JANETTE OKE

If you have young children, "quiet" rarely happens. But even if you are unable to experience a quiet morning before God, ask Him to give you a quiet heart to hear Him. Then you will have peace *and* quiet.

Continual Conversation

There is not in the world a kind of life more sweet and delightful than that of a continual conversation with God.

—BROTHER LAWRENCE

Perhaps you find it difficult to spend hours in secluded prayer. Okay, *impossible*. So when do you pray? Throughout the day, acknowledging God, asking Him for help, praising Him for His blessings. Continually.

Trail Guide

The path of life takes many turns we can't see ahead of
time. We plan our journey in very detailed fashion, and
then end up surprised or scared by twists in the road.
Instead, what if we depended on the Lord's map and His
ability to lead us? He will navigate us safely through
because He knows the terrain.

Heav'n Is Comin'

Sweetest li'l feller, everybody knows;
Dunno what to call him, but he's mighty lak' a rose;
Lookin' at his mammy wid eyes so shiny blue
Mek' you think that Heav'n is comin' clost ter you.

—FRANK L. STANTON

Of all the ways to describe the gift of a baby, nothing expresses the sentiment better than *Heaven is coming close to you.*

Flexibility

There's the possibility
that planning is futility,
so employ flexibility,
that the fragility
of your security
doesn't cause senility.
For in all probability,
your controllability
limits your adaptability.
So live in reality
and decrease your anxiety
by adapting to
changeability—
immediately.

Crowded Kindnesses

Seek to cultivate a buoyant, joyous sense of the crowded kindnesses of God in your daily life.

—ALEXANDER MACLAREN

We've all been told to count our blessings. But this statement encourages us to rejoice over God's kindnesses—His blessings. And it implies that He bestows so many, our life is crowded with them! May we have eyes to see all of them.

Dew of Quietness

Drop thy still dew of quietness
Till all our strivings cease;
Take from our souls the strain and stress,
And let our ordered lives confess
The beauty of Thy peace.

—JOHN GREENLEAF WHITTIER

Striving eclipses serenity. Allow His "dew of quietness"
to settle over you so you may rest in His beautiful peace.

Shared Kindness

Be the living expression of God's kindness: kindness in your face, kindness in your eyes, kindness in your smile.

—MOTHER TERESA

Immerse yourself in His kindness by thanking and praising Him for His past, present, and future kindness. Then your joy over serving such a kind God will beautifully radiate from you in your expressions and actions, and you will share His kindness.

Tender Words

When you lead your sons and daughters in the
good way, let your words be tender and caressing,
in terms of discipline that wins the heart's assent.

—ELIJAH BEN SOLOMON ZALMAN

In other words, speak to your child's heart
in love, assuring him that you want God's
best for him. If the Lord has his heart,
his mind will follow.

Thanks Anyway

*Thank You, God, for this good life and forgive
us if we do not love it enough.*

—GARRISON KEILLOR

Whether on difficult days or in pleasant times,
being a mother is a "good life." Even on difficult
days and in times that aren't so pleasant, we still love
our lives and thank God for this privilege called
motherhood.

Hand It Over

Since God offers to manage our affairs for us, let us once and for all hand them over to His infinite wisdom. . . .

—J. P. DE CAUSSADE

Handing over our affairs to God means to acknowledge and trust His matchless wisdom and power to do what we cannot. When we genuinely submit our parenting efforts to Him, the results will be eternally evident.

Ask God

*Instead of making our requests of God, it is good sometimes
to ask God what He wants of us, then to pause and let
His spirit speak to our hearts.*

—PAUL TOURNIER

We know what we want God to do in a particular
situation or with a particular child. But what if we
asked God what *He* wants to do? And what if we
listened?

Winning Combination

*She opens her mouth in wisdom, and the
teaching of kindness is on her tongue.*

—PROVERBS 31:26 NASB

Wisdom and kindness go a long way in dealing
with our kids: wisdom helps us know how to
handle different situations and people; and
being kind to our children, our husband,
and others teaches our kids how
to be kind.

Greater God

If you have a special need today, focus your full attention on the goodness and greatness of your Father rather than on the size of your need. Your need is tiny compared to His ability to meet it.

—BILL PATTERSON

Where we choose to focus greatly affects our perception. Focus on the Lord, and He will prove Himself greater than your need.

Joy in the Jungle

*Life need not be easy to be joyful. Joy is not the absence of
trouble but the presence of Christ.*

WILLIAM VANDER HOVEN

Like yours, my life usually doesn't fall into the category
of "easy." Parenting seven children might even be what
some call impossible. But if we abide in Christ, we all
can have joy in the midst of the turmoil.

Beyond Expectation

Faith expects from God what is beyond all expectation.

—ANDREW MURRAY

It all goes back to just how big we perceive God to be. Is He bigger than your problem? Is He more powerful than your difficulty? Is He wiser than your dilemma? Is He capable of intervening in a miraculous way? Yes to all! Expect mighty things from your mighty God!

Always God

All that God does agrees with all that God is, and being and doing are one in Him. He cannot act out of character with Himself.

—A. W. TOZER

If your usually happy child becomes irritable, you know something is wrong because that behavior is out of character for her. But God never steps out of character. He is always the same. Always *God*.

God Remembers

If I forget,
Yet God remembers!
If these hands of mine
Cease from their clinging,
Yet the hands divine
Hold me so firmly that I cannot fall;
And if sometimes I am too tired to call
For Him to help me, then He reads the prayer
Unspoken in my heart, and lifts my care.

—ROBERT BROWNING

Take Hold

*God is the one who clasps your hand as you move
from one place to another. He is the one who has
gone ahead of you, prepared a place for you, and
will hold out His hand for you to cling to.*

—SUSAN MILLER

As you move about in your motherhood duties, picture
the Lord holding out His hand for you to grasp.
Take hold!

DAY
308

Just When

Just when you think you've finally learned patience, your child tries it. Just when you think you're done with anger, your husband manages to anger you. Just when you think you never yell, you hear a screeching sound and realize it's you. And just when you think God has given up on you, He showers you with grace and forgiveness. Again.

Linger

Our joy will be complete if we remain in His love—for His love is personal, intimate, real, living, delicate, faithful love.

MOTHER TERESA

Because He loves you, God is personally and intimately involved in your life. And since your life is wrapped up in your family, His is also. Linger in that love and you will experience His joy completely.

Always Here

Sometimes the Lord rides out the storm with us and other times He calms the restless sea around us. Most of all, He calms the storm inside us in our deepest inner soul.

—LLOYD JOHN OGILVIE

Whether He is carrying us through our circumstances, changing them for us, or quieting our hearts in the midst of them, He is *always* with us.

DAY
311

Wings

Let us be like a bird for a moment perched
On a frail branch when he sings;
Though he feels it bend, yet he sings his song,
Knowing that he has wings.

—VICTOR HUGO

We have wings of faith to carry us when the branch
bends or breaks. And because of that faith, we also have
a beautiful song to sing.

Solid Foundation

*There are lots of nice things you can do with sand;
but do not try building a house on it.*

—C. S. LEWIS

Just as a contractor pours a foundation of concrete so
the house stands on a solid base, so should we build
our homes on the immovable foundation of Jesus
Christ. His Word is sure, and it stands forever.

Beauty from Bedlam

There is no situation so chaotic that God
cannot from that situation create something
that is surpassingly good. He did it at the
creation. He did it at the cross.
He is doing it today.

—HANDLEY C. G. MOULE

Believe that the Lord is creating
something "surpassingly good"
from the momentary chaos that
is your family. That's
His specialty.

Stick to It

Consider the postage stamp, my son. It secures success through its ability to stick to one thing till it gets there.

—JOSH BILLINGS

Moms must possess a considerable amount of "stick-to-it-iveness" to be able to accomplish their tasks. Whether simply completing daily chores or persevering through the emotional and mental demands of motherhood, they stick to it till they "get there."

Beloved

When we won't let ourselves be held in the midst of our messes
by God who loves us and made us, we miss the unspeakable
joy of knowing that we are truly
His beloved.

—DEBORAH NEWMAN

Maybe you're thinking right now that if He held you in
the midst of your messes, you would be constantly held!
Relax, because you are.

Love's the Thing

*In family life, love is the oil that eases friction, the
cement that binds closer together, and the
music that brings harmony.*

—EVA BURROWS

Through tense moments, distant days, and
discordant times, love brings us round again to what
matters. It transcends life's ups and downs and holds
us together, come what may.

Goodnight

*O bed! O bed! Delicious bed! That heaven
on earth to the weary head!*

—THOMAS HOOD

If there's anything more delicious than a
creamy morsel of dark chocolate, it must be
a fluffy, pillow-topped bed with cool, smooth
sheets and a thick comforter. Ceiling fan on,
door closed, silence in the house. "Heaven on
earth to the weary head" of Mom. 'Night.

Prayer for You

Hush, my dear, lie still and slumber,
Holy angels guard thy bed!
Heavenly blessings without number
Gently falling on thy head.

—ISAAC WATTS

May angels guard you and your children and
may the Lord bestow countless blessings upon
your family. May you enjoy peaceful slumber and
awaken each day grateful to God for His peace and
provision. Amen.

Moments

Let me tell thee, time is a very precious gift of God; so precious that it's only given to us moment by moment.

—AMELIA BARR

God operates outside the realm of time as we know it. In His wisdom and goodness, though, He gives us time in segments—moments to use wisely, to enjoy to the fullest. What can you do with this moment?

Discovery

The discovery of God lies in the daily and the ordinary,
not in the spectacular and the heroic. If we cannot find
God in the routines of home and shop, then we
will not find Him at all.

—RICHARD J. FOSTER

Since family and motherhood are both daily and
spectacular, ordinary and heroic, you will most
certainly find God right where you are.

Magnify

O magnify the LORD with me, and let us exalt
His name together.

—PSALM 34:3 NASB

Magnify an object and you will observe
the fascinating intricacies of its detail and
design. Similarly, you can be a "magnifying
glass" through which your children discover
glorious facets of the Lord's personality.
They will remember what they
see in you.

Blessed Childhood

Blessed be childhood, which brings down something of heaven into the midst of our rough earthliness.

—HENRI FREDERIC AMIEL

Newness of life, enthusiasm, laughter, innocence, delight. . .children exhibit all these, reminding us of things far above our earthly existence. Perhaps another instance of the Lord drawing us to Himself.

What Counts

*Teaching kids to count is fine, but teaching
them what counts is best.*

—BOB TALBERT

Of course, children should be educated. They need to
learn academic subjects such as math, language, science,
and history. But more importantly, they need to know
the wisdom of God, for knowledge without wisdom is
vanity. His wisdom is what really counts.

Lessons

The parents exist to teach the child, but also they must
learn what the child has to teach them; and the child has a
very great deal to teach them.

—ARNOLD BENNETT

My children teach me to be gentle rather than harsh.
To give away my time, energy, and affection. And
that love without sacrifice is no love at all.

Remember

*One of the most obvious facts about
grown-ups to a child is that they have
forgotten what it is like to be a child.*

—RANDALL JARRELL

If we remember what it felt like to be four
or eight or eighteen, it becomes easier to
understand our children. When we see the
world through their eyes, we are more
patient and compassionate.

Glory of Parenthood

Parents are often so busy with the physical rearing of children that they miss the glory of parenthood, just as the grandeur of the trees is lost when raking leaves.

—MARCELENE COX

Look beyond the belongings dropped by forgetful children, clothes soiled by messy children, floors tracked by sloppy children, and behold the "glory of parenthood."

More

God has a thousand ways
Where I can see not one;
When all my means have reached their end
Then His have just begun.

—ESTHER GUYOT

Mothering takes all you've got, and it would take more
if you had it. Well, in Christ you do have more. You have
as much as you need, every moment, every day,
for His provision is perfect.

DAY
328

Hang On

When you get into a tight place, and everything goes
against you, till it seems as though you could not hang on a
minute longer, never give up then, for that is just the place
and time that the tide will turn.

—HARRIET BEECHER STOWE

Don't give up. This rough day or impossible week
or insufferable year will pass, and God will turn the
tide.

Surrender

*If my life is surrendered to God, all is well. Let me
not grab it back, as though it were in peril in His
hand but would be safer in mine!*

—ELISABETH ELLIOT

If we give our lives to the Lord then yank back
parts, we think ourselves wiser than He. Let us
truly surrender everything and know that
we are safe with Him.

Steady

The man who has no inner life is the slave
of his surroundings.

—HENRI FREDERIC AMIEL

If you have an intimate relationship with the Lord
that fulfills your desires and gives you purpose, you
will not be swept to and fro by whatever happens
to you. Because of your faith you can remain steady
through all the perplexities of family life.

Be Yourself

Learn to. . .be what you are, and learn to resign with a good grace all that you are not.

—HENRI FREDERIC AMIEL

In Christ, learn who you are and be that person. Also, admit who you are not, and stop trying to be all those people. Being *one* mom is enough work for a lifetime. Don't try to be several!

Now and Here

No longer forward nor behind
I look in hope or fear;
But, grateful, take the good I find,
The best of now and here.

—JOHN GREENLEAF WHITTIER

Treasure the good and cherish the now, for it shall
never be again just as it is at this moment.

He Sees

In perplexities—when we cannot tell what to do, when we cannot understand what is going on around us—let us be calmed and steadied and made patient by the thought that what is hidden from us is not hidden from Him.

—FRANCES RIDLEY HAVERGAL

The Lord understands your circumstances and will show you what to do. His attention is always on you.

Children

Little deeds of kindness, little words of love,
Help to make earth happy like the heaven above.

—JULIA A. FLETCHER CARNEY

Children are endearing repositories of kindness and
love. . .and orneriness and mischief! But it is their
very childishness, both sweet and sour, that makes
them such bright spots in our world.

Christmas

Whatever else be lost among the years,
Let us keep Christmas still a shining thing:
Whatever doubts assail us, or what fears,
Let us hold close one day, remembering
Its poignant meaning for the hearts of men
Let us get back our childlike faith again.

—GRACE NOLL CROWELL

DAY 336

Rich

Some have too much, yet still do crave;
I little have and seek no more.
They are but poor, though much they have
And I am rich with little store.

—EDWARD DYER

If you never gain another material possession, you are rich. If you lose all your material possessions, you are rich. Because you have a family.

Good Workers

Get up: for when all things are merry and glad
Good children should never be lazy and sad;
For God gives us daylight, dear sister, that we
May rejoice like the lark and may work
like the bee.

—LADY ELIZABETH HASTINGS

Heaven forbid that we should raise lazy,
sad children. Let's teach them diligence
and the satisfaction that accompanies
honest labor.

Prayer Time

Thank God for sleep!
And when you cannot sleep
Still thank Him that you live
To lie awake.

—OXENHAM

During those nights when you are up with a child or are having trouble sleeping, be grateful first that you are alive. Then use the time to pray for whomever the Lord brings to mind. It will be time well spent.

Nothing Compares

Mother's arms are made of tenderness, and sweet sleep blesses the child who lies therein.

—VICTOR HUGO

To a child, there's nothing in the world comparable to Mommy's arms for relaxing and drifting off to sleep. And to a mommy, there's nothing in the world comparable to the feel of her little one snuggled in her arms.

Seven Secrets of Child Training

1. Watch your children with ceaseless vigilance.
2. Maintain your God-appointed leadership.
3. Help your children to find God for themselves as early as possible.
4. Keep your children busy.
5. Lay responsibilities upon your children and see they carry them out.
6. Open the treasure house of new ideas.
7. Make home the central attraction.

—MAXWELL, AS QUOTED BY BAZ (1963)

Real Help

A maid service offers a lifetime of free cleaning.
A miniature child expert sits on your shoulder
whispering wisdom. Someone besides you
cooks dinner. Ah, nice dream. But the assurance
of Psalms 121:1–2 is real: "I lift up my eyes to
the hills—where does my help come from?
My help comes from the LORD, the Maker of
heaven and earth" (NIV).

Big Answers

*God usually answers our prayers so much more according
to the measure of His own magnificence, than of our
asking, that we do not recognize His benefits to be those for
which we sought Him.*

—COVENTRY PATMORE

Simply put, God's answers are bigger and better
than our prayers. He loves to do more than we ask
. . .because He can.

Silent

A wise old owl sat on an oak
The more he saw the less he spoke;
The less he spoke the more he heard.
Why aren't we like that wise old bird?

—RICHARDS, AS QUOTED BY BAZ (1963)

When we are silent, we can listen—to our children, our husbands, our friends, and God.

All of You

> *God never comes through the door that I hold open for Him, but always knocks at the one place which I have walled up with concrete.*

—HELMUT THIELICKE

The Lord, quite simply, wants all of you. Allow Him access to every area of your heart; for if you desire your children to surrender to Him, you must be their example.

Peer Pressure

In an attempt to help our son, at the impressionable age of seven, understand the principle of not following the crowd, his dad asked him, "If everyone was jumping off a bridge, would you jump, too?" Our son replied, "Well, if the bridge wasn't too high and the water wasn't too deep." Hopefully, that meant he would think for himself!

Christmas Gift

You can never truly enjoy Christmas until you can look
up into the Father's face and tell him you have received
His Christmas gift.

—JOHN R. RICE

Whatever family traditions you enjoy at
Christmastime, the ultimate Gift of Jesus Christ is
what gives our celebrations meaning. Let us ensure
that our children take to heart the significance of
the season.

Gift of Joy

Into all our lives, in many simple, familiar ways, God infuses
an element of joy from the surprises of life, which unexpectedly
brighten our days, and fill our eyes with light.

SAMUEL LONGFELLOW

What glimmer of joy has the Lord shone through your
circumstances, bringing brightness and clarity to your
life? Today, be especially aware of and thankful for
God's gift of joy.

Mother, Defender

A mother's love for her child is like nothing else in the world. It knows no law, no pity, it dares all things and crushes down remorselessly all that stands in its path.

—AGATHA CHRISTIE

You know the feeling that rises up in you when you think someone has mistreated your child. Think how much more passionately your heavenly Father defends you!

Mean Mom

Children often mistake our discipline or instruction for just plain meanness. There once was a three-year-old who was told to get ready for bed. She marched off to comply but stopped in the doorway, turned around, pointed her tiny finger at her mom, and declared, "You're the meanest one!" Ah, the wrath of a three-year-old is a frightening thing!

Do Your Best, Then Rest

Each morning sees some task begun
Each evening sees it close.
Something attempted, something done,
Has earned a night's repose.

—HENRY WADSWORTH LONGFELLOW

You undertake your day's tasks, bring them
to completion, and enjoy the accompanying
satisfaction. Then you take a well-deserved rest,
knowing you have done your best.

Encouragement

*Correction does much, but encouragement does more.
Encouragement after censure is as the
sun after a shower.*

—JOHANN WOLFGANG VON GOETHE

Children definitely need correction. But we should
encourage them after correction, as well as when they
wisely choose obedience. In so doing, we instill in them
a positive attitude toward correction.

DAY
352

Our Gifts

We know the excitement of getting a present—we love to unwrap it to see what is inside. So it is with our children. They are gifts we unwrap for years as we discover the unique characters God has made them.

—CORNELIUS PLANTINGA JR.

If we take this to heart, we will treat our children as the gifts they are.

Life, Love, Laughter

Life, love, and laughter—what priceless
gifts to give our children.

—PHYLLIS DRYDEN

If your family embraces love and laughter
and genuinely enjoys and appreciates life, be
grateful. And be determined always to keep
it so. Then your children will be prepared
to share life, love, and laughter
with a hurting world.

On Their Own

In the final analysis it is not what you do for your children but what you have taught them to do for themselves that will make them successful human beings.

—ANN LANDERS

From tying their own shoes to taking responsibility for their futures, they must learn to stand on their own. But most importantly, they must acquire their own faith in Christ.

Precious Privilege

When you arise in the morning, think of what a precious privilege it is to be alive—to breathe, to think, to enjoy, to love.

—MARCUS AURELIUS

You simply must acknowledge the Lord and His goodness, for it is through Him that you are able to do these things. Share your gratefulness with your family and friends today!

DAY 356

Present Help

God is not the slightest degree baffled or bewildered by what baffles and bewilders us. He is either a present help or he is not much help at all.

—J. B. PHILLIPS

Are you "baffled or bewildered" by recent events? Does life have you confused? God desires to help you. Not sort of, not sometimes, not maybe— but *always*.

Present and Future

When I approach a child, he inspires in me two
sentiments: tenderness for what he is, and respect for
what he may become.

—LOUIS PASTEUR

Parents experience the privilege of knowing
and loving their children the way they are
now, but also looking forward to what
and who they will be in the future.
It is a double blessing.

Song of Angels

The earth has grown old with its burden of care
But at Christmas it always is young,
The heart of the jewel burns lustrous and fair
And its soul full of music breaks the air,
When the song of angels is sung.

—PHILLIPS BROOKS

Small Favors

*God loves and cares for us, even to the least
event and smallest need of life.*

—HENRY EDWARD MANNING

From finding a lost shoe to helping you get to an
appointment on time, God truly cares about the small
things. Is He more offended if we ask a small favor or if
we don't ask because we think He doesn't care enough
to grant small favors?

Watch Him Answer

*Put your expectations on God and enjoy watching
Him answer your prayers.*

—JAN CARLBERG

Need some advice regarding a difficulty with one
of your children? Need extra energy to get through
your days? Whatever they are, lay your requests
before your Lord and humbly expect Him to answer
your prayers. He is faithful to hear and answer.

Good Father

God is a rich and bountiful Father, and he does not forget his children, nor withhold from them anything which would be to their advantage to receive.

—J. K. MACLEAN

Just as you never forget your children or withhold good things from them, neither does God hold back whatever is in your best interest to receive. Trust His fatherly provision.

DAY
362

Strong Will

*The difference between perseverance and obstinacy is that
one often comes from a strong will, and the other
from a strong won't.*

—HENRY WARD BEECHER

Strong-willed children receive a lot of negative
press, but maybe they're not so bad after all. Perhaps
they will persevere right on past the rest of us. As
long as their "will" doesn't become a "won't"!

He Will Answer

There is literally nothing that I ever asked to do, that I asked the blessed Creator to help me to do, that I have not been able to accomplish.

GEORGE WASHINGTON CARVER

When you ask the Lord to help you in your calling to motherhood, of course He will answer! He will fill you with power and wisdom and strength like you've never known.

Mother's Love

*The love of a mother is the veil of a softer light between
the heart and the heavenly Father.*

—SAMUEL TAYLOR COLERIDGE

A mother's love—God's magnificent and
incomprehensible love, diffused and filtered so that
it may be received and shared by the human heart.
An amazing love from our amazing God!

He Will Finish!

*And I am certain that God, who began the
good work within you, will continue his work
until it is finally finished on that day
when Christ returns.*

—PHILIPPIANS 1:6 NLT

God began the good work of motherhood in
you, and you can trust Him to bring it
to completion. He always finishes
what He starts!

Notes